Martinsville Memories

and Henry County History

Stephen H. Provost

All material © 2019 Stephen H. Provost
Cover concept and design: Stephen H. Provost
All contemporary photographs © 2019 Stephen H. Provost.
Historical images are in the public domain, except where noted.

No part of this book may be reproduced, or stored in a retrieval system, or transmitted in any form or by any means, electronic, mechanical, photocopying, recording, or otherwise, without the express written permission of the publisher.

Dragon Crown Books 2019

All rights reserved.

ISBN: 1-949971-03-1
ISBN-13: 978-1-949971-03-3

Dedication

To the residents of Martinsville and Henry County, past, present and future.
And to everyone who's ever left one home and found a new one.

Contents

Foreword   7
Introduction   11
Gas, Food, Lodging   13
Heritage   53
Community   83
Industry   117
Retail   141
Leisure   171
Timeline   205

Acknowledgments

Thank you to Stephen Mark Rainey, the Martinsville-Henry County Historical Museum, Harvest Foundation, FAHI African American Museum & Cultural Center, Bassett Historical Center, James Coleman, A.C. Wilson, Dean Johnston, Patricia K. Carter and other community members whose contributions proved invaluable to this project.

Foreword
By Stephen Mark Rainey

In early 1960, before I was even a year old, my father, who worked at the DuPont plant in Chattanooga, Tennessee, was transferred to Martinsville, Virginia. Dad had just built a house on Signal Mountain in Chattanooga, and his and my mom's best friends lived there (also DuPonters). Understandably, they hated to leave a location they had come to love, but Dad, unwilling to sever ties with DuPont — a company to which he felt intense loyalty — dutifully loaded us up and set off on this new adventure. For that first year, we lived in Monroe Arms apartments on Monroe Street, just off Thomas Heights. Then we moved into a sizable, hilltop house on Indian Trail, close to Lake Lanier. At that time, ours was the only house for some distance in either direction.

It was in that house that I — and my younger brother, born in 1964 — grew up. Over the years, more houses and people came along, and Dad added a couple of rooms and made a family room out of a portion of the basement/garage. Still, it always seemed like the house, the neighborhood, never changed that much. And until I ventured off to college, I called the house on Indian Trail home.

And you know what? It is still home. I've lived in Athens, Georgia; in Chicago; and, for the past 26 years, in Greensboro, North Carolina. But Mom and Dad remained there on Indian Trail. Dad, retired from his 30-year career at DuPont, passed away in 2001. Mom, however, still lives in the house, and being close enough to regularly visit, I have faithfully continued to call that place home.

Martinsville is my home. Growing up there in the 1960s and 1970s, I was blessed to have experienced the city during its heyday. Well-paying jobs, particularly in textiles and furniture, were plentiful. The city boasted more millionaires per square mile than anyplace else in the country. We had hotels, restaurants, movie theaters, all kinds of entertainment for kids — okay, well, we had hotels, restaurants, and movie theaters — but we youngsters made entertainment for ourselves that couldn't have been more exciting if we were living in a Hollywood movie. Martinsville was a beautiful and generally safe little city, with a top-notch education system. Although most of us took our town somewhat for granted — it was the place we knew, inside and out — I could tell from an early age that Martinsville was the best place I could hope to live, learn, and mature. In 1969, Martinsville earned All-America City status, and I remember the endless ads on radio station WMVA broadcasting that fact for the world to hear. I loved listening to WMVA. Every day on the radio, the voices of Pete Bluhm and Owen Hall, our local "celebrities of the airwaves," came on like old friends (and I had the pleasure of meeting both of them in later years). Those gentlemen in large part provided the soundtrack of my youth. We had the locally produced shows *The Swap Shop*, *Chatterbox*, and others. After dark, we had *Night Train*, which played all the current hits, and *Instant Request*, where, when you heard the opening strains of The Who's *Baba O'Riley*, you could call in and request your favorite top 40 chartbuster. Not to mention we picked up three channels on the TV — at least until 1969, when we got cable, and our channel count increased to a staggering ten.

In early 1983, after college, I moved to Chicago, where I remained for most of five years. I loved Chicago, but when the company I worked for began to crumble around me, I moved with my wife and daughter to Greensboro. Only an hour from Martinsville.

I found returning to the area kind of exciting. Dad had retired, and though he suffered from some debilitating health problems, he and Mom were both happy. They still loved their house, their friends, their church, their lives in "The Ville." Even before retiring, Dad had said he would never move away from Martinsville. And he didn't.

Of course, no town is perfect. Even in those days of yore, Martinsville always bore its share of problems. As in most communities in the U.S., there were race issues; serious economic disparity; and crime, relatively rare, yet sufficiently heinous to make national news. Despite that, Martinsville shone as an affluent, alluring location, offering so much of the best of Americana. It was indeed a special town. And in many ways, it still is, although it exists as a pale shadow of its former glory. Those industries that employed the majority of the community's population are gone. For local folks, lucrative employment can be tough to come by. Crime and drug use have increased tenfold. So much of the money that drove the city's economy during the latter half of the 20th century has become "old" money, and it no longer drives things as it once did.

Fortunately, despite chronic setbacks and an aging, diminishing population, Martinsville and its surrounding environs still offer their share of golden opportunities. Numerous budding industries. Great natural and architectural beauty. Convenient travel to Roanoke and the Triad of North Carolina. Hiking trails. A much-lauded sports center. The Virginia Museum of Natural History. The Piedmont Arts Center. The Smith River. Philpott Lake. Fairy Stone Park. So much of Martinsville's rich history has been preserved in its tree-lined streets, its historic homes and businesses, its friendly people, its local pride. There's still a little piece of heaven that calls itself Martinsville.

A year or so ago, it came as something of a shock to discover that an author of my acquaintance on social media — Mr. Provost himself — had moved with his wife (also a noteworthy author) from California to Martinsville, sight unseen, based on the town meeting their personal criteria for a new settling place. Not only that, their residence turned out to be less than a quarter mile from the house where I grew up. That Mr. Provost, in his relatively brief time in Martinsville, found the city sufficiently inspiring to write this volume is one noteworthy testament.

Happily, having nearly six decades of up-close-and-personal experience with Martinsville, for this volume I was able to offer a few personal, subjective insights about growing up here as well as a little factual history. Upon perusing Mr. Provost's work to date, I find myself in awe of how much information, both written and visual, he has collected and presented. There is plentiful information in these pages that I didn't even know. The photographs, in particular, serve to illustrate the unique character of this still alluring corner of Virginia's piedmont.

Now, this volume does not necessarily provide the full, definitive, unabridged history of Martinsville and Henry County. That would be one mammoth undertaking, countless years in the works. And as time marches on, fewer and fewer of the individuals and families responsible for shaping the city's 20th-century character remain to offer their unique and invaluable perspectives. What Mr. Provost does present with this book is an insightful portrait of the locale from the point of view of a relative newcomer, rightly struck by the treasure he has uncovered.

I certainly plan to treasure this book. And I offer my thanks to the author for the opportunity to contribute what might be considered mostly amusing anecdotes. I invite you to proceed, learn, and enjoy. Above all, if you're not a resident of The Ville, please stop in and sample all the area has to offer. There's likely far more treasure here than you think.

Aerial view of DuPont plant, c. 1960

Courtesy of James Coleman

Introduction

I came to Martinsville and Henry County in 2018, looking for a new home after living my entire life in California. My initial motivation was purely financial: The cost of living in California had become prohibitive, so relocation wasn't an option, it was a necessity. The only question was: Where? Virginia stood out right away as a place in the Goldilocks zone. The summers weren't blistering hot, and the winters weren't icy cold.

What I wasn't prepared for was the natural beauty. There aren't redwoods or deserts or towering peaks here. But it's green. *Everywhere*. Trees line rural roads and highways alike. Lightning crackles across the summer sky. Fireflies light up the night, and snow dusts the ground without demanding — for the most part — that I break out a shovel to clear off my driveway.

I'd written three history books in California (*Fresno Growing Up*, *Highway 99* and *Highway 101*), and I'd been told there was so much more history out here on the East Coast than anything I was used to in the Golden State.

I knew they were right, but I didn't know where to start.

So, why not Martinsville?

I focused on the town's iconic retailer, Globman's, in a history of department stores and shopping in 20th century America (due out in late 2020) and from there, I decided to look into the history of the town and its environs as a whole.

This book, however, is a little different than previous volumes I've produced: The emphasis is on the images. Rather than illustrating my text with photos, I approached this project from the opposite direction. I chose the photos first, and let them drive the text. That's because there's so much to *see* here. The stories are still just as fascinating, but they're told in pictures and explained in words, rather than the other way around.

I hope you enjoy this look at Martinsville and Henry County the way they were, the way they are today, and how much has changed ... but also how much hasn't. So much of the history that's made this region what it is today remains right there under our noses — if only we know where to look.

Let the scavenger hunt begin.

Jefferson Hotel, Church and Bridge

Gas, Food, Lodging

If you're traveling to Martinsville, one thing hasn't changed in the past century or so. You're likely to get your first impression of Henry County when you pull off the highway to fill your tank, grab a cup of coffee or catch some shuteye at a roadside inn.

Martinsville lies at the junction of three major highways, two of which are part of the federal highway system created in 1926 that stitched together city streets and rural roads to create such iconic thoroughfares as Route 66. More modern interstate highways have, in some areas, supplanted the older federal system. But roads from that older system remain key arteries in getting from place to place in many areas — including Martinsville.

The three main highways that meet in Martinsville are Routes 58 and 220, both part of the federal system, and Virginia state Highway 57.

Business Route 220 headed north toward Collinsville from Commonwealth Boulevard.

A look at those three highways:
- Route 58, the main east-west thoroughfare across southern Virginia, roughly parallels the North Carolina state line for more than 500 miles before coming to an end near the point where the states of Virginia, Kentucky and Tennessee converge.
- Route 220 crosses portions of Virginia and four other states: Pennsylvania, Maryland, West Virginia, and North Carolina, over nearly 1,100 miles.
- State Highway 57 runs mostly parallel to Route 58, but farther north, covering just 90 miles from Halifax in the east to Woolwine in Patrick County.

A sign on Market Street at Starling Avenue offers directions to each of the three main highways through Martinsville.

You can skirt Martinsville altogether by taking the newer 58 and 220 bypasses that run south and west of town, respectively.

But what fun is that?

The older, "business" alignments of the highways will take you directly into town, providing you with a glimpse of its charm and its history.

Business 58 enters Martinsville from the east as the A.L. Philpott Highway and merges with Highway 57 at Chatham Road, near the city limits. The two then share the same path down to Market Street and westward along Starling Avenue to Memorial Boulevard, where they hook up with Business 220 and go their separate ways.

Route 57 heads north to Fayette Street, which it follows through Martinsville's historic African-American district and northwest, passing beneath a 1916 railroad bridge as it heads toward Fieldale, Stanleytown and Bassett as the Fairystone Park Highway.

In Fieldale, it runs near what's left of an old iron bridge that crossed the Smith River, which parallels the highway there. The pony truss span was built in 1931 and replaced in 2009, but a section of it was preserved and can be seen today in nearby Fieldale Park, at left.

U.S. 57 ends in Woolwine, site of two picturesque covered bridges: Jack's Creek Covered Bridge, above, which dates to 1914, and the Clifford Wood Covered Bridge, a more recent addition on private land that dates to 1977.

MARTINSVILLE MEMORIES

Route 58, meanwhile, veers south toward another historic span over the Smith River. The concrete arch structure marks a gateway of sorts to Martinsville in the south. Built in 1927, it replaced an earlier covered bridge over the waterway, the remnants of which are still visible in the form of stone supports rising up out of the water (in foreground below).

As of 2014, more than 8,500 vehicles crossed the bridge each day.

From there, Route 220 heads south through Ridgeway toward North Carolina and Greensboro. North of Martinsville, the highway passes through Collinsville, Rocky Mount and, about an hour away, hits Roanoke.

None of these highways, however, is the oldest in the region.

Not even close.

That distinction belongs to the Great Road, a portion of which parallels Route 220 a few miles west of Fieldale as County Road 683. Not only does the Great Road predate the federal highway system, it predates the automobile. It follows an old Native American trail called the Great Warrior Path and goes all the way back to the roughly

1740. (Many modern highways follow the path of former wagon and horse paths, and the first highways were actually known as "auto trails.")

The portion that passes through Henry County was known as the Carolina Road. It wound down from Roanoke — which was known as Big Lick prior to 1881, because of the salt marshes in the area — through the communities of Ferrum, Collinsville, Fieldale and Horsepasture, en route to Salem, North Carolina and points south. It served as a supply line for rebel forces during the Revolutionary War, by which time one of the local landmarks along its course had already been built.

The home known as Hillcroft, above, can be found on the east side of the thoroughfare a little north of Dillon's Fork Road. It was built in 1760, when the road was already becoming a well-traveled path. During that decade, it's estimated that about 1,000 wagons a day could be found on the Carolina Road.

Among the features of Hillcroft was a separate "traveler's room" where colonists could stay the night without bothering the owners.

As the automobile began to supplant the horse and buggy shortly after the turn of the

20th century, excitement filled the air. Adventurers wanted to know how far and how fast these new "horseless carriages" could go, so they set out to test their mettle on what passed for highways in those days: rutted trails and narrow roads. Mostly, they were dirt, but if they were lucky, drivers would come upon sections of a compacted, broken-stone surface called macadam.

One such adventure was the Glidden Tour, an annual trek founded by telephone pioneer and automobile enthusiast Charles Glidden. In 1902, Glidden and his wife, Lucy, became the first people to circle the globe in an automobile. Then, two years later, he became involved in the American Automobile Association's National Reliability Run — a sort of "Great Race."

Different auto companies were invited to enter, in competition with one another, for publicity and money. Glidden supplied the latter: a $2,000 prize (together with a trophy), and the tours thus became associated with his name.

One such tour, involving eight cars, passed through Martinsville in 1906 for the purpose of staking out a National Highway between New York and Atlanta. This was no easy feat, considering the "road" conditions: It took seven hours just to get from Roanoke to Martinsville — roughly a one-hour drive today — and the average speed was about 10 miles per hour.

C.P. Kearfott and M.E. Hundley in front of the courthouse. Kearfott's Drug Store was one of only two places where gasoline was available in Martinsville during the 1906 Glidden Tour.

An article in *Horseless Age* described some of the challenges facing tour drivers that year: "Tires are beginning to show the effects of the continued abuse to which they have been subjected. There is a good deal of pumping at the checking points, evidently to replace air lost through slow leaks, which many tires have apparently developed."

In an era before service stations, gasoline was available in Martinsville at Kearfott's

Drug Store or Hairston & Townes Garage, which stored it in a 55-gallon drum and dispensed it via a small hand pump.

The *Horseless Age* article, however, questioned the efficiency of some engines, musing that "it would be interesting to know what proportion of the oil supplied to the motors in this tour is used for lubrication and what fraction is vaporized and converted into smoke. ... Some cars in this run produce such volumes of bluish white smoke when leaving the controls as to completely obscure their surroundings, momentarily at least. This morning in the garage, it was at times almost impossible to see distinctly any distance."

Subsequent tours in 1910 and 1911 also passed through the area, en route to Jacksonville, Florida.

The U.S. federal highway system wasn't created until 1926, and early highways were mostly cobbled together from country roads and city streets. Since they were privately funded by "associations," they often zigzagged this way and that so travelers would pass within sight of the businesses that sponsored them. *The Automobile Blue Book* of 1920 described portions of Route 685 (shown at left) as following a path through Martinsville roughly along today's U.S. 220 and State Route 57: At Ridgeway, you'd fork right at the post office, then bear left and follow the curve across the rail line through a long covered bridge (possibly over the Smith River parallel to the current concrete span on Route 220).

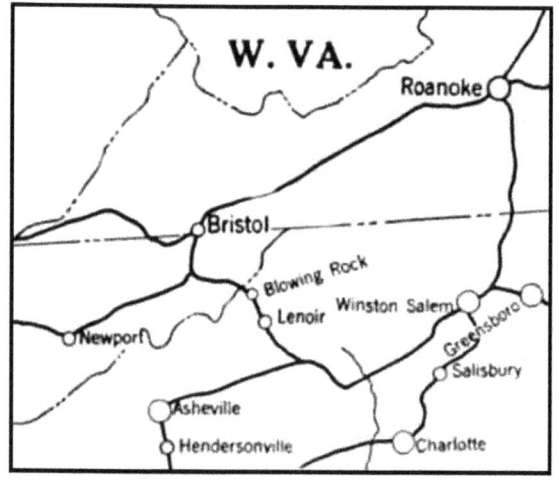

Eight miles later, you'd fork right again over a railroad bridge, go a half-mile farther and bear right onto Starling Avenue. From there, you'd turn left on Church, turn right and take the "left-hand diagonal road immediately beyond" to Main Street. You'd keep right on Main past the courthouse, then turn left onto Fayette and head toward Fieldale.

Conditions on this highway between Winston-Salem to Roanoke were spotty at best. The first five miles of the journey, the road was paved with macadam, but the next eight miles were "very poor ungraded clay," followed by "graded sand-clay to Rocky Mount."

MARTINSVILLE MEMORIES

Poor road conditions were nothing new for Virginia, where travelers had been dealing with washed-out, torn-up wagon trails throughout the 19th century. At that time, major roads were run by private companies, which charged tolls to those who used them.

These roads were called turnpikes, a name derived from their use of toll gates consisting of a turnstile: a vertical pole and two crossed bars. Perhaps most prominent of these was the Valley Turnpike, which followed the Great Road southward through the Shenandoah Valley. It began in Martinsburg, West Virginia, and continued south to Staunton, covering roughly 93 miles. (There's even a community called Pikeside just south of Martinsburg.)

Tolls were collected every five miles, and traveling the road wasn't cheap: In 2019 dollars, it would have cost just short of $100 to get from one end to the other in 1840. But it was used primarily for commerce, not commuting or sightseeing. Some of the money went to maintenance and improvement — plans called for the length of the road to be macadamized — but the owners of the pike were in it to make a profit. They sold 60 percent of their stock to the public and the rest to the Commonwealth of Virginia.

Lodges and taverns sprang up along the road in an era when road laws had nothing to do with red lights and turn signals. Instead, it was illegal to lead a bear on a public highway or, if you were on foot, to run across a bridge. You had to walk, and if you didn't, you'd have to pay a $5 fine.

The Valley Turnpike Company was doing all right until the Civil War came along. Then, suddenly, the road became a key transportation artery for the military. Troop movements wrecked bridges and tore up the road. Not only that, but the Confederate government paid only a quarter for every toll dollar the company would normally have charged. And at war's end, the company found itself saddled with $20,000 in worthless Confederate bonds it had purchased during the conflict.

After the war, railroads drew commercial traffic away from the turnpikes, depriving them of their biggest source of revenue. Some fell into disrepair, and the damage got worse for those that survived, such as the Valley Turnpike, with the arrival of automobiles: Cars were even tougher on the road than wagons had been, and operating the roads became cost-prohibitive. So, in 1918, "The Pike" was converted to a state road, with the last toll being collected on August 31, and the road became part of new State Route 3, the state's main north-south highway.

Hairston and Townes

Watt Hairston, right, loved cars. And he could afford them. His father, a major in the Confederate Army, was a member of the wealthy Hairston clan that owned Beaver Creek Plantation north of town, and Watt was his sole heir. He brought the first automobile to Martinsville when he purchased a Cadillac in 1905, and he didn't stop there, later acquiring two more cars, including the Winston Six Touring Car seen here.

Benjamin Townes, left, started the city's first garage, on Fayette Street, to service Hairston's cars. Hairston was a good customer, but not a particularly safe driver. When he brought one of his new cars into town, the vehicle struck a bystander as it came around the corner at the courthouse square. Fortunately, the man was only slightly injured. According to one tale, Hairston once paid a double fine for speeding on his way out, assuming that he'd be speeding again when he returned from wherever he was going. He died on May 23, 1916 at the age of 39 ... in an auto accident.

MARTINSVILLE MEMORIES

Five years later, Route 3 was changed to 33. It included not only the old Valley Pike, but continued along the old native trail south to Roanoke — a course later taken by U.S. Route 11. Then it veered southeast before heading south again toward North Carolina, roughly tracing the route later taken by U.S. 220. The latter covers the old road just south of the section pictured above in one of the longest straightaways on any Virginia highway. A short section of this old road remains, above, between Ridgeway and the Smith River Bridge. (The inset photo, courtesy of A.C. Wilson, shows how this section used to look, before it was cut off by modern Route 220.)

Route 33 was used until 1933, before the designation was dropped because it was deemed redundant to the newer federal highways.

Gas

Near the venerable Hillcroft, on the other side of the Great Road, you'll find another, more recent relic: a rectangular cinder-block gas stop with a red line painted across the top, just above a faded three-leaf clover and the words "Cities Service." You know it's old because Cities Service abandoned the clover symbol in 1965, when it changed its name to the more streamlined Citgo.

An old Cities Service station on the Great Road, and a modern Citgo on Route 58 east of town, where Route 57 veers north at Chatham Road.

MARTINSVILLE MEMORIES

You can find other old service stations in the area, as well.

In fact, there used to be more gas stops in and around Martinsville than there are today. At one point, Texaco alone listed 16 dealers in Martinsville, eight in Bassett and Stanleytown, and two more in Ridgeway. Esso and Gulf both were major players in the local market, too. As of 1960, Esso — which would later become Exxon — listed seven stations in Martinsville, one in Collinsville and another in Ridgeway. The next year, Gulf counted a similar number: five in Martinsville, one in Villa Heights, one in Bassett, one at Bassett Forks and one in Horsepasture.

Gradually, stations moved away from the city center. In 1940, Uptown Martinsville featured a Gulf station on Church Street next to the Chief Tassel Building, Town Clock Gas at Church and Bridge, and a Shell station just a short distance west on Church. All are gone today, but a few old service stations can be found around town, if you know what you're looking for.

The building that once housed a Gulf Super Service is still there at 201 W. Church Street. And the former Fulcher's Gulf Service is still standing at 724 Memorial Boulevard. Down the road, where Memorial meets Church and Fayette, stands a former station with an Art Deco design, below. Several stations operated at that busy three-way

intersection at various times, but this is the only building that remains there.

Just off the courthouse square in Martinsville, you can find a pair of old stations where Liberty, Depot, Franklin and Jones streets all meet. The former Esso station that now houses a jewelry store called Merridale Designs sits just to the east of Franklin and Depot, while the other old station can be found in the pie-piece-shaped wedge between Franklin and Jones.

Patricia K. Carter, owner of Merridale Designs, has been at the former location since 1991 and shared the building for the first three years with Bill Wiseman, a World War II veteran who served in Australia, India and England and owned the station in the 1960s.

"He met his wife at one of the D.C. parties," Carter recalled. "They used to have dances in the D.C. area, and people from southern Virginia would go up there on buses. He was driving for Standard Oil (which owned the station), and he did a buy-in to operate it under his name."

The building itself, she said, dates to the 1920s. It originally had a service bay to the south and three huge tanks to store fuel behind the building. She also remembered a Coca-Cola machine that operated by going around in a circle.

Although Wiseman and the owner of the station across the way were rivals, they were glad to cooperate when it came to protecting their property. When a string of robberies hit service stations in the area, the two owners developed a sort of mutual-defense pact.

"Service stations were being robbed between the '50s and '60s, and they were both carrying guns," Carter said. "If (Wiseman) thought he was being robbed, the other station owner would come over with his gun," and vice versa.

The station was just up the road from the Tultex textile plant run by Bill Franck, which has since been converted into an office complex and job-training site on Franklin Street.

Franck died in 2015 at the age of 97 and may have owed some of that longevity to the exercise he got when it snowed in Martinsville.

"He had his Jeep and his plow, and one year he plowed the parking lot (in front of the station) for free," Carter remembered. "How many people have a millionaire plow their parking lot?"

MARTINSVILLE MEMORIES

These two gas stations stood across the street from each other at Franklin and Liberty streets. At bottom is a painting of the Wiseman Oil Company building — now Merridale Designs — as it looked during its heyday in the 1960s.

Bottom image courtesy of Patricia K. Carter

The building at 308 West Church Street, top, was once a Sinclair station. Center: Workers demolish an uptown station (photo courtesy of A.C. Wilson). At bottom is a former Amoco station on Memorial Boulevard that was owned by W.D. Frith, whose Dixie Pig restaurant was — and is — right next door.

MARTINSVILLE MEMORIES

Old gas stations also can be found in nearby communities. Roughly five miles north of U.S. 58 on State Route 57, a wooden cartoon cutout of a gas station attendant waves and smiles at motorists who pass by in front of Leatherwood Grocery, at left, which has been there since 1930.

A restored Shell station is among the attractions in Fieldale, where the owner has amassed a large collection of vintage memorabilia that's on display inside. The station features an old phone booth and 1953-model gas pumps, with prices set to 18 cents a gallon for regular and 23 cents for premium. When this photo was taken, there was an old A&P sign in one of the station's front windows and a Big Boy in the other.

The station was restored by R.B. Hundley, who took on the project after retiring as publisher of the *Franklin News-Post*, a position he held for a quarter-century.

Food

These days, many gas stations come accompanied by convenience stores. You can fill your tank and get a bite to eat inside while. In at least one instance, however, gas and food crossed paths in a different way: You can't get gas at the Third Bay Café on Spruce Street, but it used to *be* a service station (see photos above; bottom photo courtesy of the café). To be precise, it was a Sunoco station that stood on the site long before the supermarket, shopping centers and other gas stations sprang up around it.

Later owners converted it into a restaurant and a garden center, and the current owners took over in 2007.

A longtime mainstay of the area was a restaurant called The Hut on Route 220 in Collinsville, where you could order "Carmen's delicious Country Club Buffet, featuring Southern fried chicken, baked ham (and) a variety of taste-tempting vegetables." The restaurant described itself as "the chalet of good food and relaxing atmosphere."

The Hut eventually changed hands, but the building was still there in 2019, and the business was still an eatery: Los Norteños Mexican Restaurant.

Another restaurant that's still around is Skip's, which serves breakfast and lunch on Starling Avenue. Skip Moore, pictured below, learned the restaurant business from his uncle, then got into it himself in 1987 when he began running the 58 Grill in Horsepasture. That restaurant burned down in a fire 12 years later, and Moore moved to Martinsville — not far from his current location — for a couple of years before heading up to Fieldale in 2000. As of 2019, he'd been in his current location for a decade.

Moore attributes his business' success to "good prices on the menu" and personal service: He makes it a practice to go out on the floor and say hello to customers as they're eating. "I kind of go out and speak to people," he said. "I go out and greet them. We're kind of small, so I'm able to do that."

Not far away, on Memorial Boulevard, is another longtime breakfast and lunch stop, D&A Café — which had been in business for 43 years as of 2019 — was serving up fare that includes hot dogs, chuck wagon sandwiches, pinto beans and onion rings. Owner Marvin Allen, who started the business with partner David Draper, said the best thing about his business is meeting people.

"I won't serve you nothin' I wouldn't eat myself," he said. "We keep it perfect. I like to see people smile."

Frith's Dixie Pig Barbecue, also on Memorial, has been around even longer, dating back to 1954. W.D. Frith built the original Dixie Pig building in for Taylor Rumley, who also at various points owned Ayers Sandwich Shop and several other restaurants. Frith took over the business himself in 1959, and eldest son Gary now runs the place with youngest son Danny.

The elder Frith also owned the building next door when it was an Amoco service station for several years.

Dixie Pig started out in a slightly different location: in the middle of what's now the parking lot. That building had a much less permanent feel than the current brick structure, which went up in its place in 1985.

On any given day, you can find Danny down behind the store, turning pork shoulders on the wood-and-propane cooker — a process he said takes about 10 hours. Salads, chicken and pies are among the items available alongside the signature pork offerings on the menu. But the most popular item?

"You aren't gonna believe it, but it's the hot dogs," said Gary Frith. "We've had them for years and years and years."

Jesse Jones hot dogs, to be exact — which also happen to be the official hot dogs of Martinsville Speedway. (D&A Café serves them, too, and both establishments make sure the public knows it by displaying big red-and-white banners out front).

The original Dixie Pig building, courtesy of Gary Frith; below, the neon sign still lights up today, and Danny Frith works the grill.

MARTINSVILLE MEMORIES

Downtown, one of the popular places to eat was the Astor Café, above. The building at 31-35 East Church was constructed in the mid-1930s. The café was more than an eatery. It was a gathering place for social and service groups such as the Kiwanis Club, American Legion, Exchange Club, Rotary Club, Junior Chamber of Commerce and Martinsville Baseball Association, to name a few.

When a place was needed to host a turkey dinner honoring 40 caddies at Forest Park Country Club in 1938, Astor's banquet room was the venue of choice. There were even dances held in a ballroom.

For a quick bite to eat, there's always been fast food. In the '50s and '60s, drive-ins were all the rage, and the Martinsville area had plenty of them — most of them along Route 220.

Warren's Drive-In on Route 220 offered "curb and table service" of "Virginia's finest hickory-cooked barbecue." Park Mor Restaurant and Drive-In, on the Memorial Boulevard segment of 220, also had "real hickory cooked Bar-B-Q" on the menu, along with "Southern fried chicken, steaks and chops." At the north end Collinsville, also on 220, was Jan's Dutch Boy Drive-In.

Jan's is still there, though with a different name. So is Ridgeway Drive-In, which opened in 1976 on Main Street, just off Route 220. The Pepsi sign in the parking lot and the placard menu fixed to the front of the building are echoes from an earlier time. Menu items range from ham sandwiches to hush puppies, from pecan pie to pinto beans.

Ridgeway Drive-In, left, and the former Jan's, now Taqueria La Juquilita, below.

Gone is the Park Mor, which served its first customers in 1951. It really was a *restaurant* and a drive-in. In 1964, it bragged that it had "not one ... not two ... but three spacious dining rooms" in addition to its drive-in facilities.

The main floor seated up to 65 people, with the newest ("and most popular") Charcoal Loft upstairs able to accommodate nearly twice that many.

There was a bandstand, and customers could even cook their own steaks over an open charcoal pit.

More recently, Sonic operated a drive-in on Starling Avenue in the 2000s, but it went out of business, leaving the building empty and vines to overtake the former sign, below.

Burger Chef, a fast-food chain that started out in 1954 in Indiana, opened a franchise in Collinsville 11 years later, selling Big Shef and Super Shef burgers to local residents on Route 220. The chain already had 350 locations by the time it opened across from the Holiday Inn, serving up 15-cent burgers and milkshakes for the same price

At its peak in 1972, Burger Chef had 1,200 locations, second only to McDonald's 1,600. It eventually sold out to Hardee's, and the last Burger Chef closed in 1996. The chain was known for its gaudy signs, such as the one pictured above, in New Mexico. The Collinsville Burger Chef ultimately became a Boost Mobile outlet, at top.

Burger Chef sign photo Library of Congress.

MARTINSVILLE MEMORIES

A former Dairy Queen drive-in building, left, is also still there, at 806 Memorial Blvd., but these days, it's occupied by a business that specializes in mailing and packaging.

Back in '62, you could get a shake there for 20 or 30 cents, depending on how much of the chilly treat you could handle.

You could also get a burger there, as the Dairy Queen had opened a year earlier in partnership with a Little Nugget Drive Inn that shared the building. Long before McDonald's introduced its Quarter Pounder, the Little Nugget was offering quarter-pound Giant Primeburgers, complete with lettuce, tomato, mustard and onions (or relish) for 35 cents. That was twice as much as some competitors were charging for a burger, but if you dropped by on Fridays, you'd get a free Pepsi with your order and could buy an order of fries for a dime — half the normal price. Still, the price was cheap by today's standards.

And that wasn't the only sign of those different times. In 1961, employment opportunities were limited: A "help wanted" specified a "refined white woman with nice appearance."

Dairy Queen no longer has a presence in Martinsville, but the same can't be said for Hardee's, which had three Martinsville sites as of 2019, including this one on Memorial Boulevard.

When it first came to town in 1964, the chain built a drive-in at that same location, on Memorial at Bridge Street. The $125,000 franchise was one of 21 planned as part of Hardee's Virginia expansion. It already operated or was building 67 drive-ins in eight southeastern states but was just four years old at the time, having gotten its start in 1960 in Rocky Mount, North Carolina.

The new building was designed to look like a Chinese pagoda, and the menu was limited, featuring "charco-broiled" hamburgers and cheeseburgers, fries and apple turnovers, along with beverages.

It would be more than three decades before Hardee's would merge with West Coast-based Carl's Jr. and adopt that chain's smiling star as its symbol. Fifty-five years later, the pagoda design at Memorial and Bridge is long gone — as are the 15-cent burgers that were standard in the early '60s.

McDonald's burgers were 15 cents, too, and the Virginia-based Kenney's chain charged the same price for its signature item. Bill Kenney opened his first Biff-Burger franchise in an old Roanoke Dairy Queen in 1958, latching on to a chain that had started in Clearwater, Florida. (BIFF stood for "Best In Fast Food.") But it wasn't long before Kenney branched out on his own, opening up a series of Kenney's restaurants and serving up burgers dipped in "secret sauce."

MARTINSVILLE MEMORIES

To compete with McDonald's, Hardee's and Burger Chef, he dropped the price of his burgers from the 19 cents Biff-Burger was charging to the standard 15 cents. Many burger joints of the day — such as Burger Chef and McDonald's, with its running tally of how many millions of burgers it had sold — used huge gaudy signs on the roadside to attract motorists. Kenney's was no exception. It featured a big downward arrow pointing toward the building, which had a distinctive A-frame design.

Such a building still exists on Memorial Boulevard south of Starling Avenue, although it's been painted gray and incorporated into a used-car dealership (see previous page). The sign out front no longer features the big Kenney's display on top, but retains the distinctive rectangular area where letters can be placed to change what's being advertised.

At its peak, Kenney's expanded to a chain with 52 locations across Virginia and West Virginia, including a dozen in Roanoke Valley. But the business gradually declined until just 18 remained when Kenney declared bankruptcy in 1980. Three were still open under different ownership as of 2012, *The Roanoke Times* reported.

Even after he left the restaurants behind, Kenney kept selling his secret sauce at Kroger in southwest Virginia, donating all the money he earned to Habitat for Humanity.

Not all Kenney's locations used the A-frame design; some opted instead for a boxier look, such as the building now occupied by The Daily Grind at Church Street and Cleveland Avenue. One of the business' owners said the building used to house a Kenney's Chicken location, and indeed, the building appears almost identical to a Kenney's Chicken ~ Hamburgers restaurant in Lynchburg.

The Martinsville Daily Grind started out in 2011 in Jefferson Plaza at Church and Bridge, but the coffeehouse moved to its current location two years later because the owners wanted a drive-thru option.

Walsh's Chicken and More moved to a different location, too. But it didn't move by choice: The original building on Starling Avenue next to Sparky's convenience store burned down — along with the restaurant's kitchen equipment — in a 2015 electrical fire that caused $500,000 in damage to Walsh's and $150,000 to Sparky's.

Sparky's closed briefly but later reopened. Walsh's, however, was ruled a total loss and had to be demolished.

That didn't keep the business from starting over, though: Less than two years later, it reopened in a smaller space at 24 West Church Street, next to the big public parking lot across from the post office uptown.

Walsh's had been in business on Starling since 1971, when it was founded by Nelson and Emily Walsh. At least one memento from the original site survived the blaze that gutted the yellow building with the gabled roof: a painting of a chicken sporting a toothy grin, which hung behind the counter there. An artist had presented the restaurant owners with the painting in the 1970s, and it had survived a previous fire in 1988, too.

After the fire, local artist Charles Hill paid tribute to the original location with a larger-than-life mural of the smiling chicken on the wall that the Sparky's store had once shared with the business. As of 2019, the old sign in the parking lot of the original restaurant remained standing next to a telephone pole at Starling and Aaron, with a canvas sign underneath it directing customers to the new location.

There, they could order chicken in various forms, including a gizzard box, drummetts and even a 50-piece dinner. The "more" in the restaurant's name included selections such as burgers, sandwiches, hot dogs, corn dogs, catfish, clams and jumbo shrimp.

MARTINSVILLE MEMORIES

A mural of Walsh's mascot, a grinning chicken, now adorns the side of Sparky's that once faced the restaurant's original location. Below the chicken is a painting of Walsh's original building, the way it looked before it was gutted in a September 2015 fire. At left, the sign still stands at the original location.

Lodging

Driving through Martinsville late in the day meant you might need to stop for the night. And that meant you'd need a place to lay your head.

In the early days, that meant a trip to central Martinsville, where hotels like the Jefferson, the Henry and the Martinsville offered overnight stays. The Henry Hotel went up in 1921, the Jefferson, seen at bottom, in 1927, and the Martinsville, around 1930.

The Henry, at right, was recently refurbished in a $3.2 million project that created 25 apartments and four commercial spaces.

Touted in the press as "one of the greatest assets in Martinsville and Henry County" when it opened, it was designed by the same architect who laid out the plan for the Beverley Hotel in Staunton.

MARTINSVILLE MEMORIES

The similarity between the Henry and the Beverley is apparent when you look at them.

Martinsville residents owned the Henry at the outset, buying stock in a corporation created to build the hotel. But public ownership ended during the Depression, when many stockholders sold their shares to generate much-needed cash. By 1933, the hotel had become part of the Grenoble hotel chain. It weathered the hard times and added 12 rooms, along with a banquet room, in 1940.

Not only did it host a variety of civic and service club meetings, the Henry also welcomed guests such as TV journalist Edward R. Murrow and the father of actress June Lockhart, a regular on TV's *Lassie* and *Lost in Space*. A new operator took over in 1950 and ran the hotel until it closed in 1966.

By that time, the era of the motel was in full swing, with more visitors to the area opting to bypass downtown and find lodging along the highway instead.

There were a number of places from which to choose.

The Fairystone Motel, above, on Route 220 in Collinsville, had 30 air-conditioned units and, if that wasn't enough to cool you off, a swimming pool, as well. Other amenities included telephones, a TV, combination tub/shower and a playground, with a restaurant right next door. All this a mile and a half north of the Martinsville city limits.

The Gardner Lee Motel was south of the city, across from the Martinsville Speedway, and right next door to the Starlite Restaurant, the "Home of Good Steaks." The Starlite offered six private dining rooms and a large banquet room, and its doors were open from 7 a.m. to 11 p.m.

At another point in time, the Gardner Lee was branded as a Travelodge, with 34 units, two pools, a restaurant, conference room, phones and color TV. In 2019, the motel was doing business as Travel Inn.

Ridgeway's proximity to the speedway made it a perfect place for the motel industry to set up shop, catering to the large crowds of race fans who inundated the city when NASCAR came to town twice each year.

MARTINSVILLE MEMORIES

King's Court in Ridgeway hasn't changed much since the postcard at top was printed in 1958, although the sign these days is different.

But perhaps the most distinctive motel in the area was (and is) the Dutch Inn in Collinsville. The motor hotel and adjoining restaurant were described as "a real Dutch Treat for the American traveler." Amenities included a pool, tap room, bedside remote control for lights and drapes, and a "bell captain" — an in-room contraption with a built-in refrigerator that dispensed "tasty snacks, candy and other treats at the touch of a button!"

In the mid-'70s, you could rent one of the Dutch Inn's 102 guest rooms for $13.50, single occupancy, $18.50 for two and $40 for the penthouse suite — inside the motel's giant windmill.

That windmill was a landmark that would certainly have attracted the attention of travelers coming into town from Roanoke in the north, but it wasn't, it turns out, the only one of its kind. In fact, there was a chain of Dutch Inns operating in such diverse locations as Miami and Lakeland, Florida; San Juan, Puerto Rico; Washington, D.C.; Hendersonville, North Carolina; and Galilee, Rhode Island.

In 1975, the company announced plans to build "one of the largest hotels in the United States" in Atlanta: "a monumental achievement ... 45 stories high to dominate the skyline and affording breathtaking vistas of the city and surrounding areas." An architect's rendering of the planned skyscraper didn't include a windmill, such as the distinctive one that graced the inn at Collinsville (and in other locations).

But the old local windmill isn't there anymore. It burned down in a 2001 fire that also gutted one wing of the hotel, leaving 30 to 35 workers without jobs as the owners scrambled to rebuild. Rebuild they did, and the Dutch Inn remains — with a new windmill, as part of what's now the Quality Inn chain. The original (left, in a 1982 photo by John Margolies/Library of Congress) and new windmills are seen below.

MARTINSVILLE MEMORIES

If you wanted to stay a few miles outside of town, you could try the Fieldale Hotel, although it was used mostly as a boarding house for Fieldcrest Mill employees and construction workers. Because of this, it was one of the first buildings in the town to be completed, in 1917. Most of those who rented rooms there were family members of the mill workers, who came to visit them in town.

The name of the place was changed a quarter-century later to the Sycamore Inn, and the hotel was eventually reborn as the Blue Ridge Apartments (bottom photo).

Another building up the road served a similar function, but it housed female mill workers rather than men. "The Dormitory," as it was known, was finished in 1920, and the name was changed nine years later to Virginia Home. It featured an open dining room and served as a social hub, serving up family-style dinners from the 1940s until 1979.

By 1996, its days as a boarding house were done, and it reopened in 2011 as the Virginia Home Inn (top photo, below).

Both places have a bit of a ghostly feel to them, as if speaking to us now in echoes from an earlier time. So did the old Broad Street Hotel in Martinsville, which has been only a memory for years now.

The two-story building, seen in the vintage postcard below, included a distinctive wrap-around porch on both floors. It started out as the Lucy Lester General Hospital, an establishment set up by Dr. Morton Hundley, a member of the Bassett family, who married Kate Black in 1927.

Kate was Hundley's second wife; he had been left a widower when his first wife, Lucy Gaines Brown, older sister of Rives S. Brown Sr., died three years earlier. (We'll hear more about the Browns in the next chapter.) But Hundley himself died of pneumonia on a trip to Switzerland with Kate just after Christmas in 1928. She took over the hotel upon his death.

"Way back when, it was a hospital and became a hotel later, I think in the early 20th century," author Stephen Mark Rainey recalled. "We used to go to the restaurant there when I was a young 'un.

"It was a *very* haunted place to my young mind. Old with lots of shadows, an upstairs that disappeared into darkness, a parlor with a portrait of 'Miss Kate,' (Black) the owner. She was a stern old woman, but she seemed to like me. I was better behaved than all those other little kids!"

If it was haunted, perhaps it was the ghost of Morton Hundley who roamed the halls, in search of the bride he'd left behind. Or maybe it was the ghost of a patient who'd passed away in the hospital.

Then again, it might have been the specter of Horatio D. Winn. The Aug. 7, 1928 edition of *The Henry Bulletin* reported that Winn, "one of Martinsville's most highly respected and esteemed citizens," had been "found dead in a bath room at the Broad Street Hotel by Mrs. James R. Winn, the proprietor."

(She was, in fact, his niece, and he'd been making his home with her for seven years, having lived in Martinsville for 26 years, since the death of his wife.)

The article continued: "A physician who examined him was of the opinion that he had been dead for several hours. Although he had been suffering with light heart attacks for several years, he seemed to be enjoying unusually good health. Only the evening before, he had attended services at the Church Street Primitive Baptist Church, of which he had been a faithful member for about 22 years."

Another possibility: Perhaps the old hotel was haunted because it was next door to the former McKee Funeral Home, which still stands, below.

Haunted

The Broad Street Hotel isn't the only Martinsville locale reputed to be haunted. According to one account, the courthouse itself may be haunted by the ghost of a jurist known for handing down particularly harsh sentences. Judge Malcolm Hugh MacBryde Jr. died in 1969, but when Debbie Hall arrived at the courthouse to put up historical displays for a festival, she heard footsteps in the locked courtroom upstairs. She called out, but received no response ... except for more footsteps.

Another Martinsville resident wrote online about John Redd Smith Elementary School in Collinsville, above, which closed in 2018. The author wrote that "you can ask anyone who goes there, and they could tell you of at least one encounter. You can experience temperature changes, shadow figures, names being called, moving and disappearing and appearing objects, voices, and much more."

A former Ridgeway resident posted: "I would walk my dog outside at night" near Martinsville Speedway, "and I would always feel like something was watching me from the woods. Occasionally my dog would stand firm and duck her head and start growling at nothing, then the hair on her back would stand up."

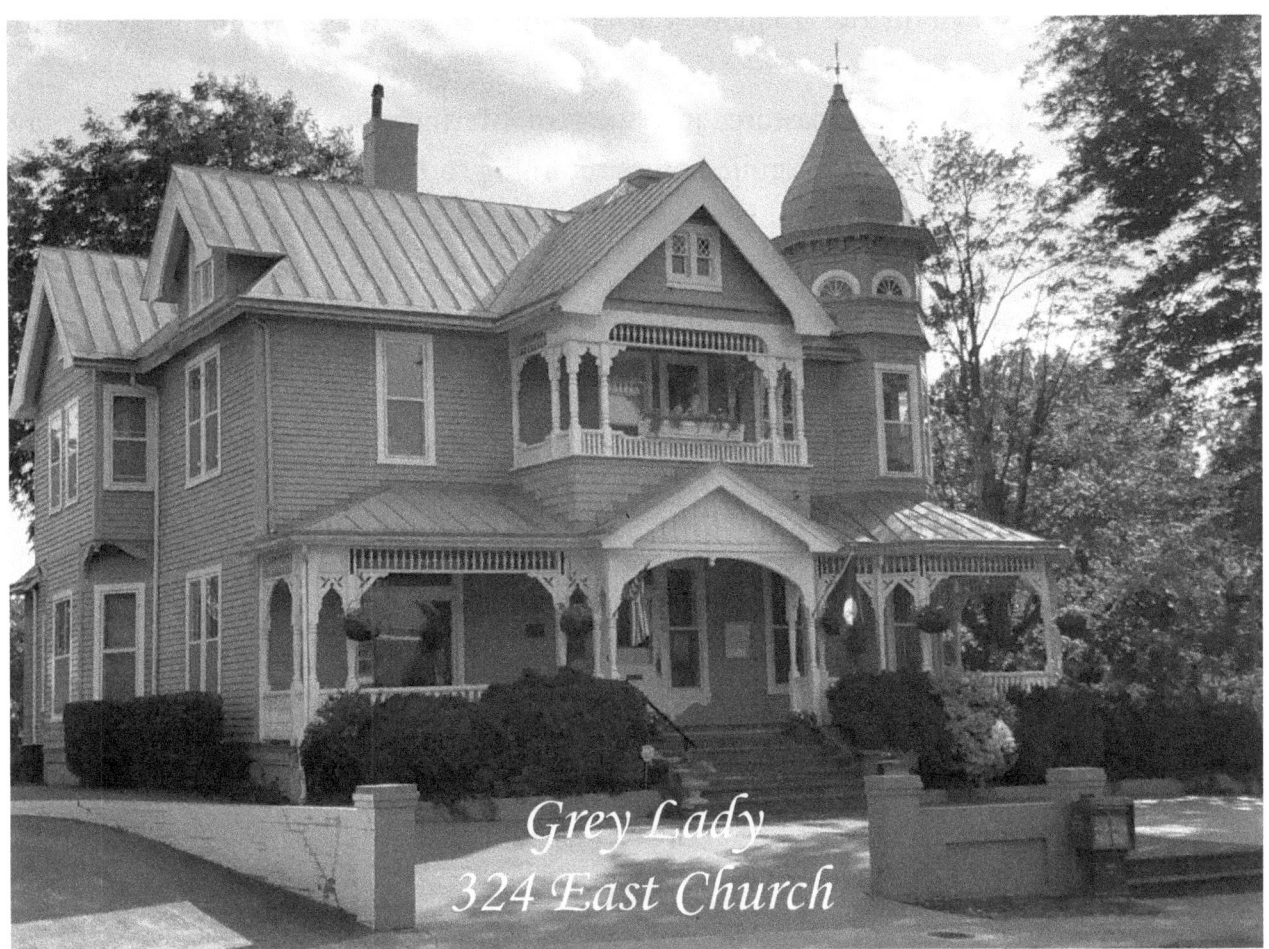

Heritage

The Martinsville area has more than its share of historic homes. Drive around, and you'll find red brick almost as far as the eye can see, with columns guarding the doorsteps of great mansions and more modest homes alike.

Some of the homes date back a century or two, while others are newer additions built in similar style. A few of the older ones once belonged to pioneers who settled here in Martinsville's early days.

On the pages ahead are photos of some of the more noteworthy homes in the area, such as the John Waddey Carter House, affectionately known as "The Grey Lady," above. The Queen Anne home can be found at 324 East Church Street in Martinsville, just outside the uptown district. John W. Carter built it in 1896 as a wedding present for his bride, Mary Kizziah Drewry.

Carter, a native of Horsepasture, just west of Martinsville, had obtained his law degree from the University of Virginia before returning to Henry County. There, he built a thriving legal practice and eventually served as mayor of Martinsville. His daughter, Ruth Carter Whitener, lived in the home until she passed away in 1987. Today, it serves as headquarters for Rives S. Brown Realtors.

Wedding Cake House
308 East Starling Avenue

G.T. Lester didn't want his pipes to freeze. His solution? Bake a wedding cake. Or, rather, build one.

The "Wedding Cake House" earned its name for obvious reasons. Lester built the three-story structure at 308 Starling Avenue, west of Market Street, with more than 3,200 square feet of living space ... but only one closet. Maybe he didn't have many clothes, but he certainly could have afforded them. Lester had money in tobacco and was also the force behind Lester Lumber. So, he could afford to import white brick from England to create his masterpiece.

Being wealthy, Lester didn't want to use an outhouse, but he also didn't want to deal with the problem of frozen pipes in winter, when Martinsville can dip into the 20s and even the teens, on occasion. So, he put his bathrooms and the heating system in a square at the center of the home, insulating them from the elements. Each room in the house had five walls, one of which was shared with the central square, providing each with a direct source of heat during the winter.

The house is unique, but it's not the only "wedding cake house" on the East Coast. Others can be found in Charleston, South Carolina; Eufaula, Alabama; Kennebunkport, Maine; New Orleans, Louisiana; and Savannah, Georgia.

Beaver Creek Plantation, 1300 Kings Mountain Road

Beaver Creek Plantation was built by George Hairston, who belonged to one of the largest slave-holding families in the South.

Completed in 1776 on a grant of 30,000 acres, it was rebuilt in 1837 in the wake of a fire. Three wings were added later in the 19th century.

The second-floor rooms are nine feet tall.

The ruined brick building seen below is a stone's throw from the main house, which stayed in the Hairston family for two centuries.

The mansion subsequently became the headquarters for Carter Bank and Trust.

The Hairstons were so successful that one writer referred to them as "the Rockefellers of the old South." Beaver Creek was just one of 45 plantations the family owned in four states — 11 of them in southern Virginia.

George Hairston also built a house (with a tavern inside!) in Martinsville on Courthouse Square sometime in the 1790s. The home was later converted into the Stevens Hotel, and remnants of it — described in the National Register of Historic Places as "two hand-planed mantels and a deeply molded door surround" — remain in the current structure on that site: the Byrd Building. Today, it's the oldest standing structure in Uptown Martinsville.

Byrd Building, 35 Jones Street

Other local Hairston mansions are nearby. The earliest, Marrowbone, was built in 1749 in Ridgeway south of town. Hordsville, built in 1836 in Stanleytown, stands across from Bassett High School. In nearby Pittsylvania County, between Martinsville and Danville, near the North Carolina state line, lie the remains of the Oak Hill mansion. Built in 1825, it was destroyed by vandals in a 1988 fire.

Hordsville top (photo by author) today; Oak Hill, above, in the 1930s (Library of Congress).

Marrowbone in Ridgeway.

Other Hairston plantations, now only memories, lent their names to communities such as Chatmoss and Leatherwood.

George Hairston's granddaughter, Bettie, was courted by her cousin, none other than J.E.B. Stuart, the Confederate general for whom the town of Stuart is named. He wrote her a number of flattering letters, and may even have requested her hand in marriage. In the end, however, she wound up marrying another cousin instead (John Thomas Watt Hairston, Watt Hairston's father) ... although she couldn't bring herself to part with the correspondence from her earlier suitor.

Speaking of Stuart, Route 58 west of Martinsville is also named for him.

The Hairston name lives on, as well.

Like many early plantation owners in the region, the family used slave labor to farm tobacco, as well as cotton. By one estimate, they had 10,000 slaves, some of whom produced famous descendants. Among them: basketball star Happy Hairston, a ferocious rebounder who helped the Los Angeles Lakers string together a still-record 33 straight wins en route to an NBA title in 1971-72. Three generations of Hairstons played Major League Baseball, and Jester Hairston was the first black conductor for the Mormon Tabernacle Choir. Carl Hairston, who attended Martinsville High, played in the NFL from 1976 to 1990 for the Philadelphia Eagles, Cleveland Browns and Phoenix Cardinals.

Hairston slave Sam Lion's memory lives on as a street name in the southeast section of Martinsville. According to legend, Lion was an African chieftain taken by slavers along with 150 others and brought to the United States. He supposedly earned his English name because of his courage — and that courage would be his undoing.

When an overseer beat him for clearing a path *around* the hills in the area, rather than over them, Lion issued an icy cold warning: "If you beat again, I kill."

The overseer just laughed and, the next day, he whipped Lion for stopping to pick up a chain he'd dropped.

But Lion turned on the man and shouted, "Didn't believe?"

Then, he promptly picked up his ax and swung it mightily, killing the man.

Lion fled and managed to elude the authorities for three years by hiding in the forest and sleeping in caves. He was finally caught and hanged in Martinsville's public square.

The street that bears his name, Sam Lion's Trail, is said to have been one of the trails he cut while working as a Hairston slave. Developer Rives S. Brown Sr. chose the name when he carved out a new neighborhood called Forest Park during the Great Depression.

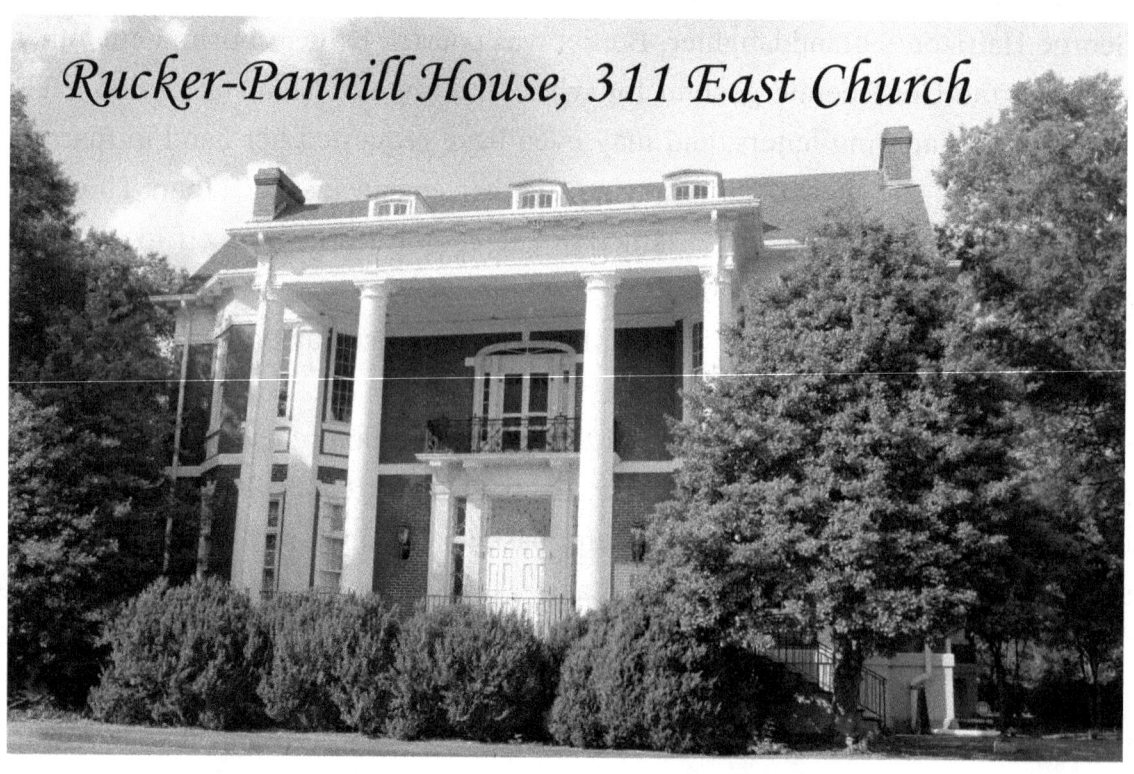

MARTINSVILLE MEMORIES

The Rucker-Pannill House, also known as Oak Hall (not to be confused with the Hairston estate, Oak *Hill*), now serves as the parish hall for Christ Episcopal Church, just one door to the east. Completed in 1920, it replaced an earlier home on the same site that had been built in 1906 by tobacco baron Benjamin Stevens but was destroyed by fire in 1917. The flames had consumed not only the house, but Stevens' collection of artwork and antiques.

Enough of the original three-story structure was saved, however, to be incorporated into the new house, including brick walls and two-story window bays.

The house took its name from Stevens' son-in-law, Pannill Rucker, for whom the original home was built along with Stevens' wife and daughter. Textile manufacturer William Pannill, a later occupant, called the home "Scuffle Hill" after the estate of Martinsville namesake Joseph Martin. Developer Rives S. Brown Sr. also lived there at one time.

Another noteworthy estate, Bellevue, can be found off the Joseph Martin Highway in Ridgeway. It was built in 1783 by Maj. John Redd, a frontier soldier in the Revolutionary War who took part in the siege of Yorktown.

Bellevue
3637 Joseph Martin Hwy.

These two buildings on Starling Avenue both have historical significance. The Kennon Whittle House on Starling Avenue just off Market Street, left, was built around 1925. Cornerstone Apartments, above, were built in the 1940s to accommodate an influx of workers at the new DuPont plant.

MARTINSVILLE MEMORIES

Portions of the concrete cornice atop the brick wall around the Lester estate were converted into benches at Lake Lanier.

The building at top was built in 1914 at 209 East Main Street to serve as a carriage house for the Henry Clay Lester mansion (inset) — except there was no Main Street there at the time. Main ended at what is now Lester Street, and the Lester estate covered a large tract of land from Church Street on the south across Main, where the mansion stood, and west to Clay Street, James Coleman said. Main was later extended.

Lester, a major player in the late 19th century plug tobacco industry, was also the first president of First National Bank in town. While the carriage house still stands, the mansion itself burned down on Feb. 25, 1946, which also happened to be the 33rd anniversary of Lester's death.

By the time Lester died, the tobacco industry that had helped make him rich was in decline, and new businesses were taking its place: furniture and, shortly after that, textiles. Martinsville was also growing: It nearly doubled in size from 1900 to 1920, and again between 1920 and 1930. That created a ready market for builders and developers.

Nearly two decades before Lester's death, he and his wife "Big Lucy" Brown Lester had adopted two of her sister's five children: Rives S. Brown Sr. and

Rives S. Brown Sr. and his son, Rives S. Brown Jr. (inset).
Courtesy of James Coleman

"Little Lucy" Gaines Brown. Rives Brown ultimately built the Rives Theatre and a Kroger market next door on land that Lester had owned. He also built the Chief Tassel building on Church Street, a few blocks to the west, and went on to develop the nearly 2,000-acre Lanier Farm — also owned by Lester — into a master-planned community known as Forest Park and Druid Hills, starting with lots around Mulberry Road.

Brown founded Rives S. Brown Realty, which his son, Rives Brown Jr., took over on his death in 1951.

Coleman's connection to all this? Not only does he run the company the elder Rives founded, he also married Brown's granddaughter — yet another Lucy. Their two children are named Rives and Lucy, too. In an interesting turn of events, after his first wife passed away, Coleman married the great-great-granddaughter of Henry Clay Lester's brother.

MARTINSVILLE MEMORIES

Mulberry Road, Forest Park

This page and the pages following show estates on Mulberry Road, a section of town developed by Rives S. Brown Sr. in the 1920s and '30s.

MARTINSVILLE MEMORIES

MARTINSVILLE MEMORIES

MARTINSVILLE MEMORIES

Out on J.S. Holland Road in Spencer, east of Martinsville, is the King House, built in the 1830s by tobacco and grain farmer Camillus King, whose sons Jeremiah and Thomas both served with the Confederate Army during the Civil War.

Thomas King, a lieutenant in the Confederate cavalry, was taken captive by Union forces and was one of some 600 soldiers (dubbed the "Immortal 600") held as prisoners of war in Charleston Harbor, South Carolina. In 1865, he was released from custody and returned to Henry County, where he became Commissioner of the Revenue.

The King House, above, was at the center of a plantation with a slave population of more than 100, some of whom are buried in a servants' cemetery on a hill by Horsepasture Creek, some distance behind the house.

Jeremiah King's fourth son, also named Thomas, was born on the farm in 1888 but left home at the age of 25 to enter the field of banking in West Virginia and, later, at Marion National Bank in Virginia, where he served as vice president. His brother John became a physician at Radford, and another brother, Clarence, also entered banking.

The estate, meanwhile, passed out of the family.

An even more noteworthy estate, Grassdale, can be found not far from the King House along Spencer Penn Road.

The estate lies on land owned by the Spencer family, who settled there in the 1780s and who made a fortune in tobacco during late the 19th century. The Spencers were already wealthy by that time: In 1860, they owned 2,400 acres worth $50,000 — or more that $1.5 million in 2019. But they were just getting started. Shortly before that, Daniel H. Spencer began farming tobacco, and he'd recently opened the Spencer & Dillard Tobacco Factory with George Dillard.

There, a crew of 31 workers produced 113,000 pounds of tobacco worth $27,300 in 1860 (equivalent to nearly $850,000 in 2019 dollars).

Grassdale, 187 Spencer Penn Road

The profits enabled Spencer to build Grassdale (originally known as "The Homestead"), and his son David W. Spencer soon joined the company — which was ultimately renamed D.H. Spencer & Sons. Their brands became household names, and their factory's location, on Fayette Street near the courthouse in Martinsville, only enhanced their visibility.

But as famous as the Spencers were for their tobacco, in May 1886, they become known for something else entirely: a gunfight on the streets of Martinsville in which nine people were shot. The confrontation took place just five years after the famed gunfight at the O.K. Corral in Tombstone, Arizona, and was just a deadly: Three people lost their lives in each showdown.

The catalyst for the bloodshed in Martinsville appears to have been an editorial in *The Henry News*, submitted anonymously by attorney William King Terry. The piece made fun of a vote by Town Council member Peter Spencer and the mayor, C.B. Bryant, to deny a tax complaint from a pair of fertilizer agents. Terry turned up the heat May 15 by distributing a scathing circular around town that further criticized the pair. According to historian Tom Perry, Spencer responded the next day by enlisting the help of another attorney to produce a poster of his own that likened Terry to a jackass.

Things began to move quickly from there. On May 17, Terry got wind of Spencer's circular and printed yet another flier, daring his critics to meet him face to face. He then called for backup from his two brothers, Ben and Jake, who arrived in Martinsville on the train.

That evening, Terry was hopping mad. He and his brothers waited outside the Spencer tobacco plant until Peter Spencer emerged along with the rest of the workers at the evening whistle.

The Terry brothers approached from one direction, and three Spencers — Peter, J.D. and George — from the other, meeting halfway between the factory and the Mountain View Hotel, which stood where Fayette Street met the courthouse square.

William Terry grabbed his pistol and demanded an apology.

J.D. Spencer called for calm, suggesting that the matter be settled at a time and place when no bystanders' lives might be endangered. He warned that the Spencers had arranged to have five gunmen present in case the feud should escalate.

Some police officers had taken similar precautions: They'd seen Terry's circular and shown up at the factory, hoping to stave off any trouble.

But despite their best efforts, there *would* be trouble.

In her 1925 *History of Henry County,* Judith Parks America Hill described Peter Spencer as a lifelong bachelor who was "loyal to his friends." His friends, likewise, were loyal to him. One of them was his business partner, Tarleton Brown, who belonged to another successful tobacco family: He was the owner of Brown's Tobacco Warehouse, and his father, Frederick Rives Brown, had been the original maker of Log Cabin Chewing Tobacco.

(If the name Rives Brown looks familiar, it's because Tarleton Brown was also the father of Martinsville Rives S. Brown Sr., and the grandfather of Rives S. Brown Jr., the two men who developed the Forest Park and Druid Hills sections of the city.)

The Richmond Dispatch described what happened next:

"The difficulty seemed almost certain to be amicably settled for the time being, when some indiscrete person fired a pistol." According to Perry, that person was Brown, who fired a shot at Jake Terry. Ben Terry then fired back, hitting Brown. "Thereupon followed a regular fusillade," *The Dispatch* reported. "At least a dozen revolvers flashed in the air. The death-dealing missiles flew thick and fast, rarely missing their prey. Every man stood his ground with nerve and grit that would do honor to the Romans. In the space of two or three minutes, nine men hit the earth. All fell in a radius of ten feet. At least three dozen shots were fired."

Jake Terry died on the spot after being shot in the side. His two brothers were hit, as well: William Terry died several weeks after the shootout, having been hit in the shoulder near the spinal column. The bullet was believed to have punctured a lung.

Ben Terry survived despite having been hit twice, in the neck and the bowels. Peter Spencer recovered, too, after a bullet hit him in the right side, struck a rib and came out his back. Two bystanders, J.R. Gregory and Sandy Martin, were shot and killed. Two police officers, Hugh Dyer and B.L. Jones — who also happened to be a saloon keeper — were injured.

The only legal penalty levied over the fracas was a $20 fine assessed against Ben Terry for carrying a concealed weapon.

Dyer would survive the shooting to serve as police chief in Martinsville and, later, Roanoke. Tarleton Brown also survived and lived until 1895, a year after his son and third child, Rives S. Brown was born. Tarleton Brown's wife died six years later. So, Brown's sister and her husband, Lucy Brown and Henry Clay Lester, raised Rives and an older sister.

This is the same Lucy for whom Lester General Hospital, aka the Broad Street Hotel, was named. The older sister she adopted was also named Lucy. So, to avoid confusion, Lucy Lester became known as "Big Lucy" and Lucy Gaines Brown as "Little Lucy."

Henry Clay Lester, like the Spencers and Browns, had made a fortune in tobacco. The Lester family name dates back to the Jamestown settlement, where a Thomas Lester was recorded in the census of 1622. According to one account, Henry Clay Lester did so well with plug tobacco that he was able to expand into other businesses, becoming a farmer, merchant and miller. After a time, according to one account, he became the richest man in Virginia and a vast landholder. Among his holdings was Lanier Farm, a 2,000-acre swath of rolling hills and partially forested land south of Martinsville.

MARTINSVILLE MEMORIES

He left Lanier Farm to Rives S. Brown and Little Lucy, who married Dr. Morton Hundley of the Bassett family. But she died in 1925, and he remarried Kate Black. Her brother started Rives S. Brown Real Estate three years later. Lanier Farm became the site for Brown's developments.

Spencer-Penn School, 475 Spencer Penn Road

As for Grassdale, Mary Spencer Buchanan — sister of Peter, J.D. and George — owned the estate for several years and, in 1910, donated land for a three-room wooden school building to serve children in grades 1-7.

The estate was owned by the Penns, yet another tobacco-growing family in the region. Two other Spencer sisters married members of the Penn family: Lizzie wed Rufus Penn, and Annie married Francis Reid "Frank" Penn, who owned the F.R. Penn Plug Tobacco Factory in Reidsville, North Carolina. (He sold it to American Tobacco in 1911).

Frank and Annie's son, Thomas Jefferson "Jeff" Penn, built the Chiqua Penn Plantation in Reidsville and also owned Grassdale for a time. In 1926, he donated $25,000 to build a new school where the old wooden school had been constructed, complete with five classrooms and an auditorium. It opened to the primary grades in 1927, with the wooden building being converted into the community's first high school.

The Spencer-Penn School closed in 2004 and became a community center, site of family reunions, meetings, performances, athletic events and the Spencer Fair.

Although the Spencer estate remains standing, the plantation built by Joseph Martin, for whom Martinsville is named, has long since faded into history. The estate, called Scuffle Hill, is not to be confused with the historic mansion on Church Street that now serves as the parish hall for Christ Episcopal Church. That home was named in honor of Martin's Scuffle Hill, but is in a different location and dates from the early 20th century.

The original Scuffle Hill was on the Smith River a couple of miles south of Martinsville, but the city wasn't the first place in Virginia to bear Martin's name. That honor belongs to Martin's Station, an outpost in Powell Valley at the far west end of Virginia — just inside where the state lines of Tennessee and Kentucky now come together. Those two states didn't exist then (no states did, of course, since this was before the Revolution, and Virginia itself was still a British Colony), and the land to the west belonged to Native American tribes.

By the time he got to Powell Valley in 1763, Martin was about 23 years old and had already served in the French and Indian War at Fort Pitt, on the site that later became Pittsburgh. He served there alongside Thomas Sumter, for whom Fort Sumter is named. But at this point, Martin's skill as a gambler equaled or surpassed his achievements as a soldier. According to his son, gambling was his favorite pastime, and he was known to feign drunkenness to make himself appear an easy mark. While at Powell Valley, he even engaged Patrick Henry in a surveying contest, in which he won 20,000 acres of land.

A different sort of contest led to his acquisition of Scuffle Hill.

In the 1760s, Martin become an overseer for one Dr. Thomas Walker, who was eager to secure acreage in Lee County for settlement — land then occupied by Native Americans. In 1769, Walker put the following proposition to Martin and a rival by the name of Captain Rucker: He would give 21,000 acres to whichever one of them managed to settle in Lee County first.

Martin got lost for a while and described himself as "completely exhausted, weak from

Joseph Martin

hunger and very discouraged" by the time he reached his destination. Despite this, however, he managed to beat his competition by nearly three full weeks. His problems weren't over, though: After he'd set up camp there, a band of Native Americans invaded his base, one of whom grabbed his rifle. After a scuffle, however, Martin wound up with the weapon, and the Native Americans retreated. He secured his earnings from Walker and used the proceeds to buy the Smith River land, naming it Scuffle Hill in honor of his scuffle with the Native American raiding party.

Henry built an estate he called Belle Monte on Leatherwood Creek in 1774, and the following year, he was made an agent for the Transylvania Company, with the authority to settle land in western Virginia and beyond. The company bought up huge tracts of Cherokee land that year, constituting roughly two-thirds of what's now Kentucky. This they dubbed the Transylvania Colony (yes, that's what they called it!) and hired none other than Daniel Boone to establish a road from Cumberland Gap into their new territory. But the colony only lasted one year. The Virginia Assembly invalidated the company's purchase of the land in 1776.

Martin's first wife died while he was living in Henry County, and he took a second wife after her death. Except she was actually his *third* wife, and he was still married to the second. Betsy Ward was the daughter of Cherokee leader Nanyehi, who had taken the name Nancy Ward upon marrying an English trader. The trader, it so happened, was already married at the time, too. And indeed, Martin justified his own bigamy by saying it was a common practice among frontiersmen dealing with Native American tribes.

Such an arrangement did have strategic advantages. Martin's relationship with Betsy Ward enabled him to gain valuable information about British efforts to incite Cherokee tribes against the colonists — efforts that he ultimately stymied. After a battle in which 176 Virginians defeated 800 Cherokee warriors, Martin returned at the head of a 50-man unit that forced the surrender of Native American settlements and the expulsion of the British agents who had established a foothold there.

In 1777, Patrick Henry — who served twice as Virginia governor — appointed Martin as agent and superintendent for Indian affairs, a position he held for 12 years, simultaneously serving in the same capacity for North Carolina for half that span. He was appointed brigadier general for the North Carolina Militia and, six years later was commissioned to the same rank with the Virginia Militia.

He was elected to the Georgia legislature in 1783. He then represented Sullivan County, North Carolina, in that state's legislature from 1784 through 1787, and was a member of the North Carolina convention that ratified the Constitution. He later served in the Virginia House of Delegates from 1790 until retiring. He died in 1808 at age 68.

MARTINSVILLE MEMORIES

While Martin had a city named after him, Patrick Henry lent his name to not one but two adjacent counties: Henry County and Patrick County, to the west.

The two-time governor of Virginia, known for uttering the famed declaration "Give me liberty or give me death!" in 1775, moved to a 10,000-acre Leatherwood Plantation near Axton four years later and lived there until 1784.

The plantation, like so many others in the area, later became the property of the Hairston family, and the estate no longer remains. But the Daughters of the American Revolution erected a historical marker at the site in 1922 that's still visible today in the shade of several trees.

The inscription reads: "This boulder marks the landed estate of Patrick Henry where he lived from 1778 to 1784. Erected by the Patrick Henry Chapter, Daughters of the American Revolution. 1922."

Cemeteries

About 430 people are buried at People's Cemetery (above), established in 1918 at the end of 2nd Street for African-American residents of Martinsville. Oakwood Cemetery at 107 Cemetery Street (below) was founded in 1883. Pictured is the Lester-Brown plot.

MARTINSVILLE MEMORIES

Even the most cursory survey of noteworthy Henry County buildings would be incomplete without a reference to the central building in town, courthouse.

The structure dates back to 1824, when it replaced an earlier courthouse on the property. George Hairston had deeded the 50-acre parcel to the city in 1791, and the first courthouse had been constructed on the site two years later from hewn logs on a stone foundation.

The structure that replaced it can be seen above, in an early photo by the pharmacist, C.P. Kearfott, whose drugstore stood across the square from this vantage point. Notice the external central staircase, which was replaced in 1929 by an interior stair.

The Confederate monument was added to the grounds in 1901, and the two cannons were brought to the property from Fort McHenry, outside Baltimore.

The photograph at left shows the courthouse in 2019. The war monument in the photo, topped by an eagle, pays tribute to local citizens who lost their lives in wars from the American Revolution to the present.

When the 1824 courthouse was built, there wasn't much else to Martinsville. It wasn't even called Martinsville then, but was more commonly referred to as simply "Henry Courthouse." The town, such as it was, consisted of eight homes, two stores, two taverns, a tanyard and a few other shops. The only two-story building, other than the courthouse itself, was the George Hairston house on Jones Street, which later became the Stevens Hotel and was incorporated into the present Byrd Building.

Town population: 84, including 34 blacks.

By 1851, a road called the Danville and Wytheville Turnpike passed through town.

As for the courthouse, the county courts continued to be housed there until 1996, when they were moved to a new location. The building now serves as home to the Martinsville-Henry County Historical Society's Heritage Center & Museum. With the help of grants from the Harvest Foundation, Henry County, and Save America's Treasures, a projected $1 million restoration project was completed for less than $200,000 in 2010.

U.S. Post Office, 1 West Church Street

Community

Schools, churches, the post office, community centers ... these are the things that tie a community together. As new towns sprang up, they were always among the first structures to appear — even if the earliest community centers were often in saloons, barbershops or around a cast iron stove in the general store. Globman's, for instance, had one of these.

Abe Globman's son, Leon, remembered: "There was a pot-bellied stove in the store for heating and cooking. Mother would cook in the store and put my sister and myself on top of the fabrics counter, and we'd sleep until the store closed."

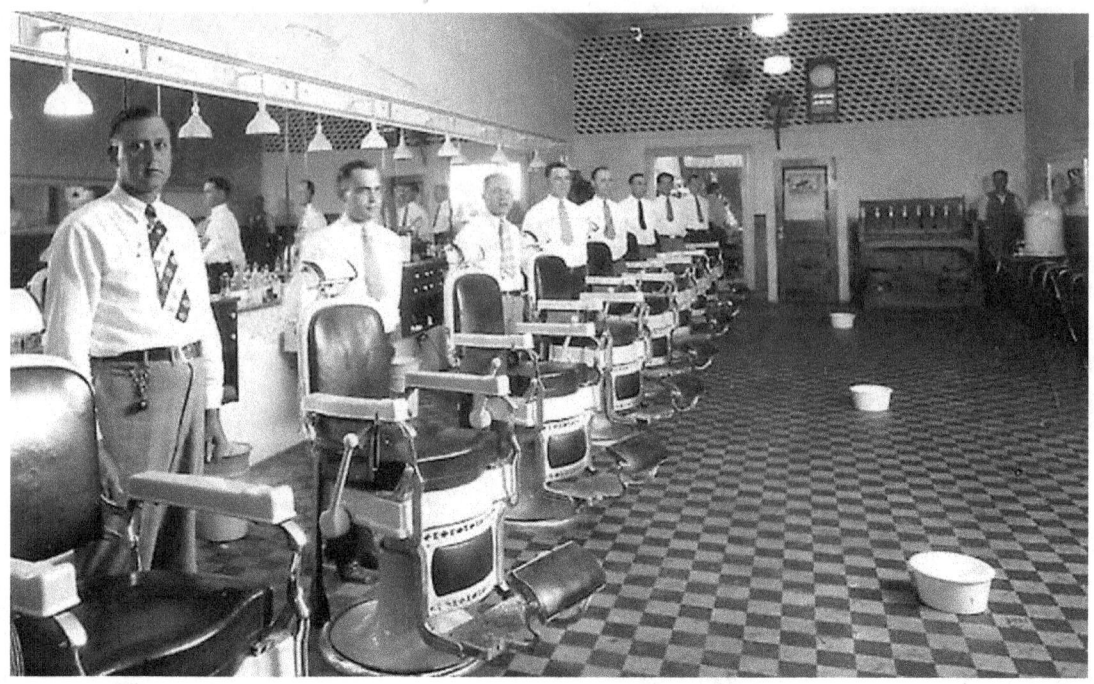

An early photo of Draper's Barber Shop on Franklin Street from the 1920s shows a staff of well-dressed barbers behind a row of chairs, waiting for customers. In front of those chairs are three white basins: spittoons, which were a natural feature of such a business in an area known for its chewing tobacco.

The current post office, at Church and Bridge streets, is an imposing two-story structure with Doric columns flanking the entrance and a cupola at the center of its roof. Built in 1939, it was part of President Franklin Roosevelt's Works Progress Administration (WPA), which lasted eight years and provided work for 8.5 million Americans in the depths of the Depression. It's an imposing structure that provides a sense of grandeur worthy of a courthouse or great mansion.

But it was not Martinsville's the first post office. An earlier structure served the same purpose on the same site, having been built in 1906. It's gone now, but an earlier satellite office, the "Little Post Office" on Starling Avenue just off Mulberry Road, remains. The building is, indeed, little: a single-story brick structure that looks like a whimsical cottage out of a fairytale. It was actually a private building, constructed by contract mail carrier John Anglin, whose home — which no longer stands — was also on the grounds.

Anglin built the Little Post Office to serve his rural route, which was known as a "star route." Contracts were awarded to private carriers at the lowest bid "necessary to provide for the due celerity (e.g., swiftness), certainty and security of such transportation." These three attributes were signified by postal clerks using three asterisks — or stars. Hence, the name "star route." Contracts typically ran for four years, and unexcused delivery failures could bring a fine as high as three times what the contractor would have earned for completing the route.

Anglin's Little Post Office continued to operate until 1917, and the building is still there today in the R.P Gravely-A.J. Lester Art Garden at the intersection, near a piece of public art commemorating Martinsville's selection as an All-American City in 1969.

Schools

Martinsville Junior High, like the Post Office, is an impressive structure that looks more like a high school. And with good reason — it once *was* the city's high school. Also like the Post Office, it was built in 1939. The new campus on Cleveland Avenue, above, replaced the city's first high school, known as The Ruffner Institute from

Library of Congress
Martinsville High School's Class of 1912.

its founding in 1871 to 1904, in honor of Henry County's first superintendent of schools.

The graduating class of 1900 were known as Marvahi (short for Martinsville, Virginia high school), a name that stuck for the school's annual yearbook.

Most early schools in Henry County were one-room log schoolhouses with gabled roofs, serving a small number of students. There was a reason for this: A state law passed in 1870 mandated that schools be in walking distance of every student in the state, and 15 years later, there were 48 schools for whites and 28 for blacks in segregated Virginia.

As populations centers grew, however, so did the schools that served them. Even in rural areas, two- and three-room schoolhouses became more common around the turn of the 20th century. These schools generally served younger students; a three-room school might have one room for grades 1-3, one for grades 4-6 and one for grades 7 and 8. By the 1920s, campuses with more classrooms were being built. Ridgeway Elementary School, below, constructed in the late 1920s, is one example.

In addition to the main red-brick building, the Ridgeway Elementary complex included a 1929 wood-frame agricultural building, along with a home economics building and a Quonset hut cafeteria, both built around 1940 for what was then a high school. The school at 380 Church Street in Ridgeway closed in 2008, with students moving to a remodeled Drewry Mason School — which also began as a high school and also opened in 1929.

Segregated rural schools for African-American children expanded gradually. Additions were made to Rock Run School near Fieldale, which began as a one-room schoolhouse in the early 1880s, and Carver Lane School in Bassett, which was built around 1920.

Rock Run School, above, closed in the 1950s. Unlike many schools built in the late 19th century, it is of wood-frame construction rather than being built from logs. It has undergone restoration but has become overgrown with trees and weeds, as has Carver Lane School, right.

Larger towns such as Martinsville had high schools, and those were growing, too. When the 1939 high school campus was built, it included a unique feature: an enclosed spiral slide tube to the ground floor that served as a fire escape.

Martinsville High has a rich athletic heritage, especially in basketball, where the boys' program has racked up 15 state championships — more than any other school in Virginia. The Bulldogs grabbed their first state title in 1958 and their most recent in 2016, when they won their games by an average of 29 points. Their other titles came in 1961, 1964, 1966, 1976, 1980, 1981, 1982, 1985, 1986, 2001, 2002, 2006 and 2015.

As of 2019, the school had also won two state football championships, two golf titles and one girls basketball crown, taking state honors more often than any other team in the eight-team Piedmont District.

Former Detroit Tigers second baseman Lou Whitaker tops the list of famous MHS athletes. Whitaker, who moved to Martinsville when he was a year old, was the American League Rookie of the Year in 1978 and a five-time All-Star, playing for the 1984 World Series champions. His 28 home runs in 1989 still stand as a record for Detroit second basemen (although Ian Kinsler matched that figure in 2016), and he ranks among the Tigers' top five players for career double plays, assists, games played, runs scored, doubles and total bases.

Shawn Moore, a Heisman Trophy finalist at quarterback for the Virginia Cavaliers in 1990, also attended Martinsville High. We went on to a professional career with the Denver Broncos, Arizona Cardinals and several Canadian Football League teams.

Another former CFL player, quarterback Sonny Wade, also went to high school in Martinsville. He spent his entire career with the Montreal Alouettes, and became the first three-time MVP of the league's championship game, the Grey Cup.

Martinsville High School's current campus.

Other communities in Henry County had their own high schools, as well. But the old Bassett and Fieldale high schools aren't used for classes anymore. Fieldale High School closed in 1965, when the new Fieldale-Collinsville High School opened roughly halfway between the two communities for which it was named (it subsequently became a middle school in 2004).

Today, the old Fieldale High campus isn't in great shape, and neither is the old all-grade school not far away. The latter school, built in 1920 as a four-room brick school, was expanded to house secondary students in 1931 until the high school was built a decade later. Weeds cover the front of the abandoned and neglected school, threatening to obscure the walkways entirely, and some of the windows are broken out.

The Fieldale All-Grade School, above, and the old high school, right.

MARTINSVILLE MEMORIES

Unlike Fieldale, Bassett still has its own high school, built in 1978 on the same road — Riverside Drive — as its predecessor, the old John D. Bassett High School. In fact, students from Fieldale and Collinsville now attend the Bassett campus.

The 1947-48 school, seen below, isn't used for classes anymore, but it is well maintained. In fact, the impressive structure, with its twin cupolas over columned entrances at either end, has been transformed into an event center. Inside, you'll find a theater that seats 585 people, a banquet room with space for 250 more, a gym that can host trade shows, a computer lab, and eight conference rooms, each with a capacity of 40 people.

The brick building was added to the National Register of Historic Places in 2006.

Martinsville, like Bassett, relocated its high school students to a new campus, with junior high pupils taking their place. The current high school opened on Commonwealth Boulevard in 1969.

Times were changing in other ways, too.

Just a year earlier, the high school had become fully integrated, as African-American youths began attending classes there after decades of segregation. The former all-black Albert Harris High School was converted into an elementary school that year, as students of color started attending Martinsville High.

Albert Harris had served as principal of the Martinsville Colored Grade School on Spencer Street beginning in 1917. Five years later, it was replaced by the Martinsville Training School — the campus on Smith Street later named for Harris. The eight-room schoolhouse was built on land donated by Betsy Hairston with the help of $150 contributions from black residents and $1,600 grant in "Rosenwald funds" — a program set up by Sears president Julius Rosenwald.

Rosenwald's goal was to set up more than 5,000 schools for black youths in 15 states across the South. One of those was in Martinsville: a brick schoolhouse just off Route 58, on the city's east side. The building, Dry Bridge School, opened in 1929. It housed four classrooms and two offices, and another building was added next door in 1958 to a campus then called East Martinsville Grammar School. The school was closed a decade later, when the district was integrated.

MARTINSVILLE MEMORIES

Dry Bridge School, 1005 Jordan Street

Martinsville's African-American population had its own community, centered on Fayette Street and the surrounding neighborhoods west of downtown. In 1960, institutional segregation was still very much alive — and not just in education, where black and white youth attended different schools.

It was the year of the lunch-counter sit-ins, which started just an hour south of Martinsville in Greensboro, North Carolina. There, four African-American college students refused to leave a Woolworth lunch counter in protest of a store policy that refused them service. The sit-ins would spread to lunch counters in five-and-dime and department stores across the South.

In one tragic case, seven black men were executed in Martinsville after being convicted of raping a white woman in 1951. Thirteen were initially charged, but the alleged victim was able to positively identify just two of them. Still, the Martinsville Seven, as they came to be known, were convicted and sentenced to the electric chair.

There was evidence of unequal treatment even in the pages of the newspaper. When the black community's most celebrated pioneer marked his 50th year in town, it was noted not on the front page — where *The Bulletin* announced a new comic strip, printed college football scores and announced an increase in building permits — but seven pages in.

In that story, Dana O. Baldwin recounted how he had come to Martinsville after graduating from medical school in Raleigh and had begun his medical practice at the suggestion of another Martinsville physician, Dr. Jesse Shackelford — founder of the Shackelford Hospital on Church Street. Baldwin became the first black doctor to serve a community that was, at the time 40 percent African American.

He did so, initially, by making house calls, often alongside Shackelford.

"And how I walked and walked," he told *The Bulletin*. "In those days, nobody came to see the doctor, and they didn't have telephones. I went to see them all over Henry County, and I walked until somebody found me an old gray mare from Finley's Livery Stable for $25 down and $25 a month. Then I would ride as far out as Stuart and Stella."

But Baldwin put down roots in Martinsville, running his practice from an office at Fayette and Moss streets "because Dr. Shackelford said I should help my people instead of seeking greener pastures."

Baldwin was not just a doctor, but a businessman, and in his early years in town, he ran first a short-lived movie theater and then an ice cream parlor in the basement of the Martinsville Hotel.

Later, he purchased a tract of land on Fayette, along the block between his old office and his new home at Fayette and Barton. There, he built a series of buildings that housed a drugstore, barbershop, grocer, billiard parlor, beauty shop, café and dentist's office, with a hospital on the second floor. It became known, fittingly, as the Baldwin Block.

Dana O. Baldwin served in the U.S. Army Medical Corps from 1917 to 1919.

Unfortunately, the entire block burned in a fire in 1929, and the $9,000 insurance payout was just enough for Baldwin to pay off his mortgage.

Still, with the help of the community, he was able to rebuild.

"I built it up again and operated that hospital for 25 years until Community Hospital was built," he recalled. "In the end, it was the only one of the enterprises that showed a profit. We charged $20 a week for a patient then."

Maternity stays could last a week and produce $35, while insured patients from the mill in Fieldale provided a reliable income in an era when many couldn't afford to pay out of pocket.

"I remember we were always glad to see (a patient) from Fieldale, because Fieldcrest was the only mill that had hospital insurance at the time," he said.

Baldwin's pharmacy served up milkshakes, ice cream and sandwiches. He opened another cinema for blacks in 1929 on the Block, premiering Cecil B. DeMille's *King of Kings* there. He later leased the 350-seat Baldwin Theater to R.S. Brown, who renamed it the Rex.

Other businesses soon sprang up in the area, such as Imperial Savings and Loan, founded in 1927, which occupied the building, above, at 211 Fayette Street. These days, it's the home of the FAHI Museum and Multicultural Center. (FAHI stands for Fayette Area Historical Initiative.)

In the '30s, Baldwin opened a motel on the Smith River that featured a swimming pool and hosted an annual dance party, or "German Ball," each June for more than four decades. James Brown, Sam Cooke, Duke Ellington and Cab Calloway were among the performers who played there.

Sandy Beach Resort was at 2399 W. Fayette, just outside town where Fayette Street becomes Appalachian Drive. A postcard invited visitors to "come and picnic with us," at a place that offered "swimming, boating (and) many forms of recreation" along with "guest rooms and concessions."

Sandy Beach operated until the 1970s. A thickly wooded area stands in the place once occupied by the resort.

Another popular gathering spot was the Paradise Inn on the west side. Built in 1946, it immediately was a hot spot for entertainment and socializing. James Brown stopped in there, too, as did Ray Charles, Diana Ross, Louis Armstrong, and Ike and Tina Turner. At various times, the two-story building also housed a beauty parlor, pool room and barbershop, with apartments for rent. There was even a roller rink on the grounds.

The business eventually closed, and the city condemned the building in 2008; the neon sign was removed in 2010. Nine years later, the structure remained in poor repair, boarded up and vacant, a silent witness to an earlier era.

Paradise Inn, 802 West Fayette

A second movie house, the 400-seat West End Theater, operated during the 1950s. These days, it's a church.

It was important for the community to have fun. Indeed, Dana Baldwin lived by the motto "Hard work never hurt anybody, but don't forget recreation."

It seemed to serve him well: He lived to the age of 91, passing away in 1972. Both his daughters became teachers, with one working at Albert Harris High School.

MARTINSVILLE MEMORIES

The Baldwin Block buildings were torn down in the 1970s. Today, the 53,000-square-foot Baldwin Building, below, occupies the block. It's home to the New College Institute, Henry County Economic Development Corporation, and Martinsville Visitors Center.

Left and bottom photos courtesy of Harvest Foundation

Dana Baldwin's pharmacy is seen in this photo from the 1930s.

Sanctuaries

Churches have always played a key role in the life of Martinsville residents, and there are plenty from which to choose. Travel down any country road in Virginia, and you're likely to stumble upon a red brick building with a steeple, spire or bell tower — with chimes such as those at First Baptist, above, that call congregants to worship.

Christ Episcopal, 321 East Church

MARTINSVILLE MEMORIES

Under British rule, the Anglican Church dominated. But after the Revolution, it lost its influence in Virginia, leaving the Baptist and Methodist churches as the denominations of choice.

By around 1960, there were 47 churches in the Martinsville city limits, run by denominations including Lutheran, Methodist, Disciples of Christ, Presbyterian, Baptist and Episcopal.

Some, of course, were bigger than others. And some were more than just a red brick building with a steeple. Among the most impressive — and one of the oldest — is Christ Episcopal Church, which was built around 1890. The congregation itself was founded in 1841 three blocks west of its current location. The church's bells, manufactured in Holland and installed in the bell tower in 1983, ring out on the hour.

First Baptist, just up the road on Starling Avenue (next to the Virginia Museum of Natural History) has an impressive bell tower of its own. It wasn't the first Baptist church in Henry County — that honor belongs to the Leatherwood Primitive Baptist Church, established in 1770.

First Baptist was founded more than a century later, in 1884, in the home of pharmacist C.P. Kearfott, who had arrived in Martinsville three years earlier.

The church's first building went up on Broad Street in 1888, followed by a larger building at Broad and Church in 1927. That church looked like a Roman temple or bank building, with its massive columns supporting a gabled front piece over the entryway, and a matching feature guarding arched windows on its other street-facing other wall.

That cruciform-floorplan church, with a central rotunda, is depicted in the postcard above. It was replaced in 1960 by the current structure on Starling Avenue, at left, and the older structure was demolished.

But a similar entryway, can still be seen on another church, First United Methodist at Main and Lester streets, below in a vintage postcard. (For the church as it appears today, see next page.) It was built in 1922, replacing an earlier church on the site.

MARTINSVILLE MEMORIES

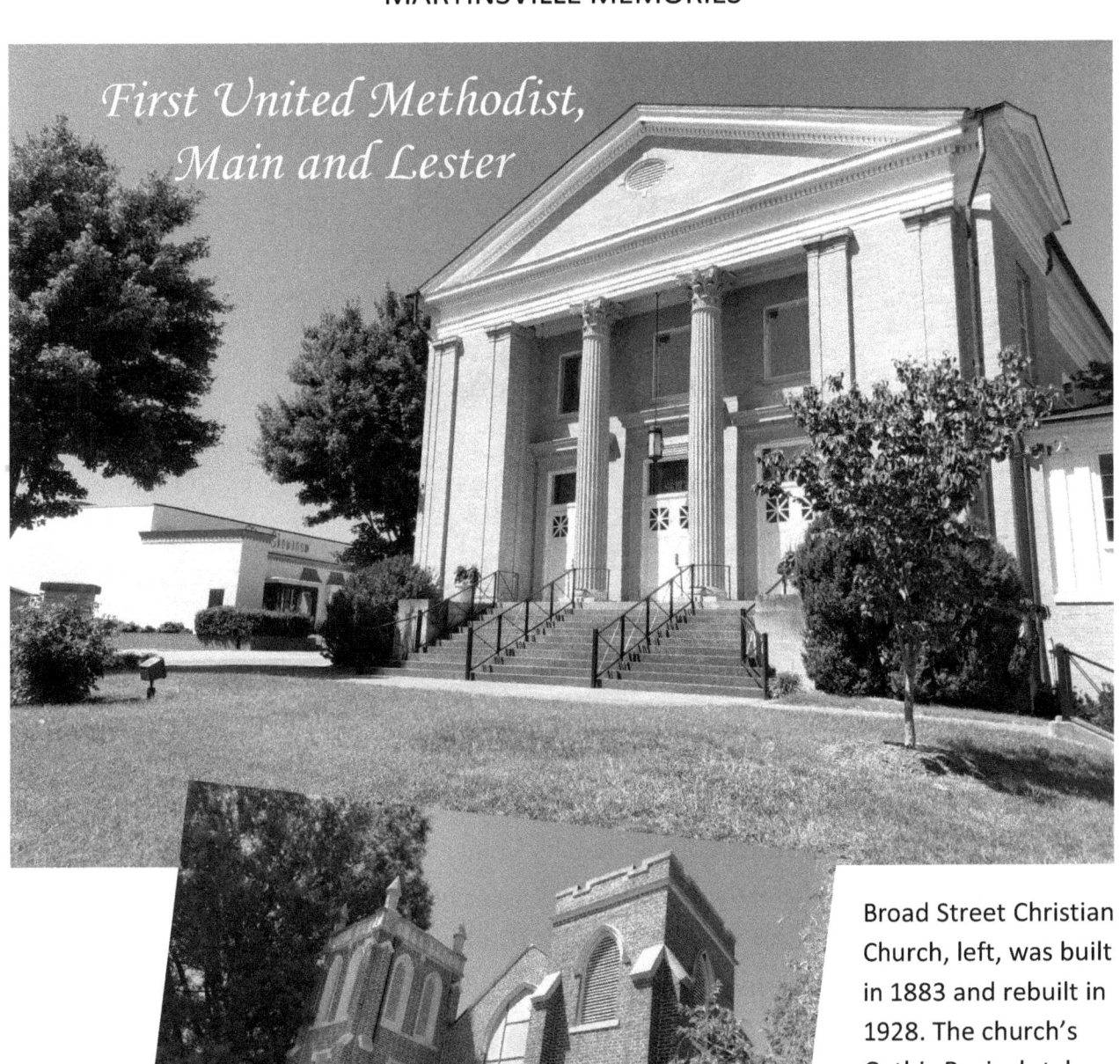

First United Methodist, Main and Lester

Broad Street Christian Church, left, was built in 1883 and rebuilt in 1928. The church's Gothic Revival style somewhat resembles the architecture of the larger Christ Episcopal on Church Street. The current structure was built for $60,000.

First United Methodist, Broad Street Christian, Christ Episcopal and First Baptist were all constructed near what is now the city center. In fact, however, all were on the fringes of the main commercial area when they were built. Sunday was, after all, a day of rest and worship, when stores were closed and worldly considerations put aside.

Other churches, meanwhile, were established along the Fayette Street corridor and served the city's African-American community.

Grace United Presbyterian Church, above, was built in the 1910s on Fayette Street. The congregation started meeting at the home of Peggy Redd in 1882, but growth quickly led it to relocate in a tobacco factory basement. Redd's home, meanwhile, became the starting point for a second church, High Street Baptist. A wooden building for Grace Presbyterian was built, but burned down, leading to the construction of the present structure.

Other early churches in the African-American community included Mt. Zion A.M.E., and Fayette Street Christian Church, which, as of 1902, was the only place in town where blacks could attend high school.

Over on Third Street, west of Fayette, the Pilgrim Missionary Baptist Church, top, opened its doors to worshippers in 1951.

The church was built with bricks that had been donated by the Martinsville Brick Manufacturing Co., founded by Dana Baldwin had founded in 1939.

The Baldwin plant, near the location of Walmart at the end of Commonwealth Boulevard, employed more than 25 people and could churn out 75,000 bricks a day.

The former West End Theater at 1002 West Fayette Street, above right, became the Divine Faith Holiness Church.

To the south (clockwise from top): First Presbyterian, in two photos, on Patrick Henry Avenue in Druid Hills; Stone Memorial Christian Church, Collinsville; St. Joseph Catholic Church on Spruce Street; Christ's Church on Spruce Street Ext.

MARTINSVILLE MEMORIES

Rural churches have included, from top, Reed Creek Primitive Baptist north of Bassett Forks at 2075 Reed Creek Drive (built c. 1850); Leatherwood Church (c. 1875) and Koehler Baptist (1936). Note the twin doors at the top two churches, providing separate entrances for men and women. Congregants still meet at the Reed Street building.

Trinity Presbyterian Church at Kingsmill Road and Harbour Street in Ridgeway, right, was founded in 1889. As of 2019, it had a membership of five people, according to its website. Below, an abandoned church building sits just across the county line in the community of Cascade, south of Axton.

MARTINSVILLE MEMORIES

Farther from town, rural churches were available as options for worshippers. Among them was the Granbery United Methodist Church in Leatherwood, above.

Originally known as Bethel Methodist, it was built in 1889 and took on the name of John Granbery, minister of the Southern Methodist Episcopal Church.

The rural church was originally illuminated by kerosene lamps on the walls and, until 1957, was heated by a wood stove. Before that, Sunday school classes were only convened nine months each year in deference to the winter chill. It's the oldest church building in Henry County to have been used continuously for services since its construction.

Not all places of worship in the area are that old, and not all serve those of the Christian faith. The Ohev Zion Synagogue on Moss Street served the area's Jewish population, which included some of the city's most prominent residents. During the early 20th century, a significant number of Jews immigrated from Eastern Europe, many of them making a living as traveling salesmen and operators of stores that sold "dry goods" — clothing and related products. These stores were the forerunners of big-city department stores such as Gimbel's, Kohl's, Rich's and Abraham & Straus, all of them founded by Jewish families.

The original Ohev Zion Synagogue, right, was built in 1929 on Moss Street between Church and Market. The synagogue later moved to a new location on Parkview, above, between Spruce and Mulberry in the Druid Hills neighborhood. The original synagogue now serves as the city's Senior Center.

MARTINSVILLE MEMORIES

Several Jewish entrepreneurs in Martinsville started their own stores, as well. The first of them was Samuel Heiner, who was born in Russia and ran a Martinsville clothing store from 1888 to 1929. He eventually operated a small chain that included shops in Bassett and Rocky Mount, along with three others in the North Carolina towns of Madison, Reidsville and Stoneville.

One of Heiner's employees, a fellow Russian-born Jew named Samuel Kolodny, worked for him from about 1911 to 1915 before starting his own store. Kolodny briefly partnered with father-in-law Abraham Fusfield — who had emigrated from Austria — in a department  store venture at 5 East Church Street, next door to the Holt's building. (It later moved up the street to 40 East Church).

Max Berlin came from Lithuania and ran Berlin's Department Store on East Main Street from 1911 to 1955. But the most successful Jewish merchant in Martinsville was Abe Globman, who founded Globman's Department Store. And it was Globman who spearheaded the effort to build a synagogue for Martinsville's 46 Jewish families.

Globman approached one of his friends in the business community for help with the $15,000 venture: Big Mike Schottland of the Virginia Mirror Company.

"I decided to move all of the store's basement housewares to a temporary location for a few months," Globman would later recall.

"For years I had been playing cards with one of my best friends, Mike Schottland, who owned a vacant place next to City Hall. So, in the morning I went to see him. We dickered for a little about the rent. I told him, 'Mike, what do you care? You'll never see a penny of it because we are building a new synagogue. … Mike Schottland shook his head in mock despair, and five months later he endorsed a sizeable rent check back to the synagogue's building fund."

The Moss Street synagogue continued to serve as a gathering place for Martinsville's Jewish community until 1960, when a new synagogue was built on Parkview Avenue.

Hospitals

Martinsville has been home to a number of hospitals, most of which no longer exist. Among them are the Shackelford Hospital on Church Street, a former Victorian mansion converted into a hospital around 1920; Lucy Lester General Hospital on Broad Street; St. Mary's Hospital, which Dana Baldwin built in 1926 above his pharmacy on Fayette Street; and Martinsville General Hospital on Starling Avenue, built in 1946.

The Shackelford Hospital was named for Jesse Martin Shackelford, a physician from the family of none other than Joseph Martin, for whom Martinsville was named. He founded Henry County's first hospital in 1895 in a wing of the house he built in his native Irisburg, southeast of town.

Shackelford's son John followed him into the medical profession, and both practiced at the Shackelford hospital. Jesse Shackelford was the first president of the Virginia Hospital Association, established in 1926, and John Shackelford pioneered the use of several new medical techniques in Henry County, including x-rays and blood pressure measurement.

MARTINSVILLE MEMORIES

Unfortunately, it wasn't yet clear how damaging the effects of x-rays could be to those who failed to adequately protect themselves. As a result, John Shackelford suffered radiation burns on his left hand that were so severe he lost the tips of two fingers.

The Shackelford Hospital, at 22 East Church Street, was at the heart of Martinsville's business district. It was demolished in the late 1940s or early '50s when Martinsville General was up and running. Today, the West Piedmont Business Development Center can be found where Shackelford Hospital once stood. Martinsville General was ultimately torn down to make way for the Virginia Museum of Natural History.

Martinsville Memorial Hospital, built in 1970 to replace Martinsville General, combined with Danville Regional Medical Center to become SOVAH Health in 2017.

Shackelford Hospital, right, on vintage postcard, and Martinsville General on Starling Avenue, courtesy of James Coleman.

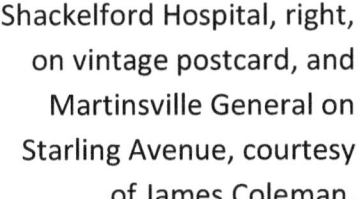

Watt Hairston Memorial Hospital, left, opened in 1919 but burned down a year later. It was named for Watt Hairston, who brought the age of the automobile to Martinsville when he purchased a Cadillac in 1905. The hospital stood on property now occupied by the Village of Martinsville (Liberty Fair) shopping center.

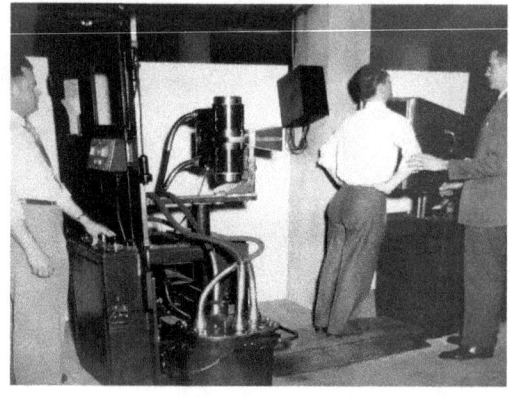

Above, a bird's-eye view of Martinsville General Hospital, on Starling Avenue where the Virginia Museum of Natural History now stands. At left, the state Health Department employs a mobile x-ray machine in Henry County in 1950.

Images courtesy of Harvest Foundation

The Arts

Big Mike Schottland's former home on Starling Avenue later became home to the Piedmont Arts Association.

Schottland was a mirror guy — he'd founded the Virginia Mirror Company in 1913 — so it was only natural he would have an interest in telescopes. He even ordered one for his home, but it wasn't just any telescope. Installed in 1940 at an observatory he built at the house, it was constructed to work specifically from Martinsville's position on the globe.

Schottland exchanged that model for an even bigger telescope a decade later, and at one time, his residence had the nation's largest privately owned telescope. Big Mike donated the first one to NASA's Lowell Observatory in Arizona, and it was used to identify more than 20,000 asteroids — one of which was named 25940 Mikeschottland in 2015.

Schottland Home/Piedmont Arts, 215 Starling

The Piedmont Arts Association moved into the former Schottland house in 1981 after spending the previous five years at DuPont's Lynwood House. The Schottland home was renovated for Piedmont Arts at a cost of $100,000. It hosts art workshops, the performing arts, exhibits and more. The sign out front was installed in 2006.

As of 2019, Martinsville had two troupes of performing artists. The Patriot Players, featuring local students and community members, at Patrick Henry Community College; and TheatreWorks Community Players, established in 2004, in the 120-seat BlackBox Theatre — the former Townes Furniture Store at 44 Franklin Street in Uptown.

Oktoberfest is held in early October uptown. The Rooster Walk Music & Arts Festival takes place each spring on Pop's Farm at 675 Hobson Road, with a companion fall festival, Brewster Walk, in Martinsville.

For the literary-minded, Martinsville has boasted its own library since 1913, when the Martinsville Women's Club bought up books to create one on the first floor of the courthouse. It later moved upstairs and, in the late 1940s, to the remodeled Andes House on Church Street, by which time its collection had grown to 6,000 books.

The current library opened in 1963 on the same site (after the Andes House was torn down) and expanded in 1986. It's now part of the Blue Ridge Regional Library, which has branches in Collinsville, Ridgeway, Bassett and Stuart.

Museums

The Martinsville area has its share of museums that preserve the area's history. In addition to the Martinsville-Henry County museum at the courthouse, there's the FAHI museum a few blocks away on Fayette Street, celebrating the history and contributions of Martinsville's African-American population.

Up the road a way is the Bassett Historical Center, whose extensive genealogical records include 10,000 family files and more than 16,000 genealogy books. Also in its archives are company collections from DuPont, Tultex, Henry County Plywood, Blue Ridge Hardware and various Bassett family industries.

Among the most impressive is the Virginia Museum of Natural History on Starling Avenue, former site of Martinsville General Hospital.

The museum moved to its current location in 2004 after spending 20 years in the former Joseph Martin Elementary School building on Douglas Avenue, just off Memorial Boulevard.

The old Joseph Martin Elementary School was home to the Virginia Museum of Natural History for 20 years.

The still-vacant elementary school building isn't small. You can see it just up the hill as you drive on Route 220, across the street from the former Kenney's Drive-In.

Even so, the new museum was a significant upgrade — and not just in appearance (it may be the most impressive modern building in Martinsville), but in terms of space. Its 90,000 square feet included 19,000 square feet of exhibit space, five times as much room as the old school provided, allowing the museum to take millions of specimens out of storage.

In fact, when the $13 million facility opened, it had a total of 21 million natural history specimens. Exhibits showcase such topics as Virginia's natural history from its beginnings to the present day; animal life in Africa; dinosaurs; the Ice Age; and ants. Research and fossil work are conducted on site, as well, with windows that allow visitors to observe the scientists at work.

There's a lecture hall, a gift shop, and a schedule that includes events such as regular science talks, a dinosaur festival and a dragon festival.

What's inside the building is at least as impressive as the building itself.

> "There is no better field in the South for the location of manufacturing enterprises than Martinsville. Its ample railroad facilities with competing lines to deep water at Norfolk cheap freight rates, superb water power, healthful climate, mild, short winters, with plenty of raw material close at hand, indeed nothing is lacking but capital, push, and enterprise."
>
> *Article in The Martinsville Standard, 1902*

Industry

It all started with tobacco.

Before the Civil War, plantation owners in the area relied on slave labor to harvest the crop, and its cultivation remained big business after the war, as well.

As Martinsville grew from a population of 300 to more than 2,000 during the 1880s, the tobacco industry grew along with it. By the turn of the century, there were no fewer than 14 tobacco factories in the Martinsville, which became known for its plug tobacco — a form of chewing tobacco pressed into a brick shape that's held together with molasses or another form of syrup. The user removes a piece of the brick, or "plug" and holds it between the cheek and gum.

Early tobacco manufacturers included Henry Clay Lester in Figsboro and B.F. Gravely in nearby Leatherwood.

The Danville & Western Railroad, known colloquially as the "Dick & Willie" reached Martinsville in 1881 and made it as far as Stuart three years later. It was the railroad that helped boost Martinsville's population over the coming decade, bringing people like pharmacist Clarence P. Kearfott, who rode the first passenger train to travel on the new rail line from Danville into Martinsville and set up his business downtown.

A vintage postcard, above spotlights the Danville & Western line Martinsville depot c. the 1920s. At left, an engine pulls cars along the D&W line.

It would be hard to overstate the impact of the railroad on industry and commerce in Henry County. Factories from American Furniture to DuPont, from Martinsville Novelty to Bassett, were all built close to rail lines or spurs. Boxcars gave manufacturers a way to ship large quantities of goods far and wide, something they couldn't do easily or cheaply via wagons traveling toll roads.

Trains also brought more people to town.

Martinsville was at the crossroads of two rail lines: The Danville & Western (originally the Danville & New River), which came to town in 1882, and the Norfolk & Western, which began service nine years later.

MARTINSVILLE MEMORIES

If you took the Dick & Willie west from Danville, you could travel south on a spur to Leaksville (Eden), or continue on the main line through Cascade to Axton and Martinsville. Other stops en route to Stuart were Fieldale — another crossroads town for the two rail lines — Preston, Critz and Patrick Springs.

The Norfolk & Western traveled down through the Shenandoah River Valley to Roanoke, then turned directly south to Martinsville, with stops in Boone's Mill, Wirtz, Rocky Mount, Ferrum, Bassett and Fieldale. After hitting Martinsville, the train went on to Ridgeway and several stops in North Carolina before reaching Winston-Salem.

Passenger service between Bassett and Martinsville continued through mid-1957.

Fire destroyed Martinsville's Broad Street Station on the Norfolk and Western in 1978. But you can still visit the Bassett railroad depot, above, which has been kept in tip-top condition. The same can't be said for the Axton station along the D&W line, which is still there (inset above), but dilapidated and barely recognizable.

The railroad gave tobacco manufacturers a way to move their crop more quickly from factory to customer, and it's no accident that B.F. Gravely (whose Leatherwood factory, dating from 1850, is seen at right) built a new factory in Martinsville right across from the D&W depot.

According to one story, a case of the common cold led Gravely to develop a distinctive blend of chewing tobacco that was flavored with licorice. As part of his regimen for combatting his illness, Gravely consumed a good deal of licorice in liquid form. He happened to be chewing tobacco at the same time, and found he liked the combination. So, he decided to make it and market it to the general public.

The Spencer family, meanwhile, owned not one but three plug tobacco companies in the 18th century. The Spencers founded the community that bears their name, west of Martinsville, and not only benefitted from the Dick & Willie Railroad — they controlled it. In addition to using their own rail line to ship their tobacco to market, they made their own boxes in which to ship it.

The Spencers were well known for brands such as Old Crow and Calhoun. In all, their factory produced nine brands of plug tobacco.

But the era of tobacco would not last forever in Martinsville. By the turn of the 20th century, the public's taste was trending toward cigarette tobacco and away from plug tobacco.

At the same time, larger companies — particularly R.J. Reynolds — had begun buying up smaller manufacturers. Reynolds snatched up

Rucker & Whitten Tobacco Co. of Martinsville in 1905. But perhaps most noteworthy was Reynolds' acquisition of its most bitter rival, the Spencer brands. Indeed, company founder Richard Joshua Reynolds had been born in the Patrick County, near Critz, just 10 miles west of Spencer.

Under a deal struck in 1903, the Spencers agreed to form a corporation in exchange for stock in the combined venture. Four years later, Reynolds — now based in Winston-Salem, North Carolina — bought up a controlling interest in D.H. Spencer & Sons of Martinsville.

Tobacco was no longer king, and the local business community was forced to turn its attention elsewhere in search of capital. Former tobacco barons such as the Gravelys and Whittens set their sights instead on manufacturing.

Specifically, furniture.

In 1902, four members of the Bassett family started the Bassett Furniture Company.

Then, four years later, former tobacco manufacturers A.D. Whitten and C.B. Keesee, started the American Furniture Company.

Two other furniture companies, Stanley and Hooker, came along in 1924, and the Gravelys started their own furniture business two years later.

Bassett was not just the first, it also became the largest — not only in the region, but in the world. A whole town grew up around the company, and its population increased to 3,000 by 1969. That was still fewer people than the company employed that year, when 4,000 worked at plants in Bassett and Martinsville, and 1,000 more were employed at smaller plants in Virginia, North Carolina and Georgia.

A *New York Times* article that year noted that there were other employers in town, citing a knitting mill and hardware producer, but also noted that members of the Bassett family sat on their boards of directors.

Another community built around the furniture industry grew up next door to Bassett. Stanleytown was named for Stanley furniture, whose founder, Thomas Stanley, would go on to serve as governor of Virginia from 1954 to '58.

Stanley actually started out working for Bassett, and when he struck out on his own, he located his factory nearby and built a company town to support it. Roads were paved, and 100 homes were built to house the factory's workers, who paid rent of $4 or $5 a month. Stanley Furniture rolled out its first collection — a dining room set that featured a buffet, server, china closet, table and chairs — in 1925, and it was an immediate success, allowing the company to expand rapidly for the rest of the decade.

Clyde Hooker, like Thomas Stanley, began his career working for Bassett. In fact, his furniture business got off to an improbable start after Hooker took a trip to Martinsville on behalf of J.D. Bassett Manufacturing. Not only was Hooker secretary and treasurer of the company, he was married to Bassett's niece, Mabel. He seemed set for a successful future in the family business.

But during that trip to Martinsville — where he had gone to see about a shipment of mirrors — Mike Schottland, the head of the Virginia Mirror Company, presented him with an unexpected proposal: Why not start his own furniture company in Martinsville?

The answer to that question was simple: Hooker estimated he would need $30,000 for such an endeavor, and that was $30,000 he didn't have. However, if the residents of Martinsville would *give* him that sum to start up the company, build a factory and hire workers, he'd consider it.

Amazingly, that's exactly what happened.

The publisher of the Danville newspaper gave Hooker 20 acres of land, and Hooker collected $28,000 from the community.

It wasn't a loan. It was an outright gift.

Or, rather, an investment.

Community leaders knew that more jobs and more industry in Martinsville would bring more money into the community — which would ultimately benefit their own businesses.

If that weren't enough good fortune for Hooker, he even got J.D. Bassett to go along with the idea, bestowing his blessing on Hooker to use the family name in the enterprise he dubbed the Hooker-Bassett Furniture Company.

Hooker's headquarters remained in Martinsville as of 2019, employing more than 800 workers on the company payroll in Virginia and North Carolina.

American Furniture also made its mark in Martinsville, starting out in 1906 with 30 employees making wooden bedroom furniture in a single brick factory.

By 1965, the company had grown to include five factories in a sprawling 20-acre complex that covered 2½ blocks downtown. A building on Lester Street at Green Street (seen on the next page), still bears the faded red lettering "American of Martinsville" above the smaller designation "Plant No. 10."

The company was riding high by the time the 1960s came to a close, boasting annual sales of more than $37 million.

Courtesy of Harvest Foundation

American Furniture employees on Starling Avenue in 1907.

Fire, however, seemed to plague the business. In late February of 1965, some 100 firefighters from nine communities converged on the oldest unit of American's downtown complex, where a fire had broken out on the third floor. It took them seven hours to bring the blaze under control, with the damage estimated by the company president at "hundreds of thousands of dollars." It was the worst fire in Martinsville since an overnight blaze in 1951 that devastated an entire city block downtown.

The company also built a massive complex near the rail line at a site bounded by Broad, Aaron and Railroad Streets. But that complex met an even worse fate in 2014, when six of eight buildings on the site burned.

Top: A vintage postcard shows the American Furniture Company plant from Railroad Street during its heyday. Above: From roughly the same vantage point in 2019.

Three years later, fire struck the same site again, setting off explosions, sending black smoke into the sky, and collapsing at least one exterior wall of a structure that has survived the previous fire. Amid the smoldering aftermath, melted steel beams stood amid the smoke as testament to the blaze's intensity.

In 2019, the site remained roped off, with bright red fire-inspection signs warning passersby that the property had been condemned and ruled unsafe: "... its occupancy (or use) is prohibited by the code official." The section of Aaron Street next to the plant was also closed to traffic. There was talk that the property, seen below, might be redeveloped as affordable housing.

Sometimes, furniture wasn't called furniture.

When you think of "novelties," your first thought is probably of knick-knacks, toys or something you might win on the midway at the fair. But the Martinsville Novelty

Corp. actually made furniture — smaller pieces such as cabinets, bookcases, coffee tables, gunracks and end tables. The factory on Rives Road, built across from a Bassett factory on the other side of the Norfolk Southern railway in 1929, initially employed 35 to 40 employees. Raw lumber went in one end of the building, and emerged from the other end as finished furniture.

In addition to the main brick building, there was a restaurant for workers at both the Novelty and Bassett factories, which also served, over the years, as a service station and store. The Bassett factory was eventually torn down, but the Novelty factory complex still stands. The 90,000-square-foot plant closed in 1995 and was eventually converted into a 60-unit apartment complex.

Martinsville Novelty, 900 Rives Road

Like Martinsville Novelty, the Virginia Mirror Company was a more specialized operation, producing, well, mirrors. The company was founded in 1913, and a subsidiary, Virginia Glass, started up in 1956. Together, they had 165 employees as of 2018. At one time, Virginia Mirror was the nation's largest mirror plant under one roof.

When furniture came along, textiles weren't far behind.

"Furniture was probably first, then textiles came along a year or two later," said lifelong resident A.C. Wilson. "The men were generally in the furniture business, but the women didn't have a place to work. So, the textiles gave them that, and the economy started thriving. ... You could have a job and get fired or quit, and after lunch you could have another job. It was a buzzing place."

Wilson would know. It was that economy that gave his family its start in Martinsville. Wilson's father, Alec C. Wilson, came to town during Prohibition and bought a house on Mulberry Road that's still in the family. His first job: to collect debts on past-due accounts run up by moonshiners. They'd go out and buy cars with big engines, which they installed small cars so they had enough horsepower to stay one step ahead of the law. But they wouldn't pay the auto companies when the bills came due, so those companies hired people like Alec Wilson to collect.

The elder Wilson eventually started the area's first small-loan business, lending sums anywhere from 50 cents to $10 for 0.5 percent interest. (Today, A.C. Wilson owns that business, Martinsville Finance and Investment Corp.)

By that time, the textile industry was already booming in the area.

Most people associate Marshall Field with the iconic Chicago department store that bore his name for more than a century. What may not be as well remembered is that his company also produced textiles — and that a lot of that production took place in Henry County. In fact, the town of Fieldale is named in honor of that effort.

Fieldale's upper section, along Marshall Way, in 2019.

MARTINSVILLE MEMORIES

In 1911, Marshall Field's acquired seven mills in Eden, North Carolina, about 20 miles southeast of Martinsville. Five years later, the company began construction of Fieldcrest Mills in the area of Waller's Ford, which had been settled by George Waller — a first cousin of Patrick Henry — in 1770. Like Stanleytown, it became a company town, designed as a semicircle around a hill, with an upper and lower section. Field Avenue curved around the base of the hill, while Marshall Way ran across the top of it, creating two intersections of Marshall and Field.

The upper section had four buildings, housing a bank, post office, grocery store and Fieldale Fruit Company. The lower section consisted of a pool hall and café, theater, drugstore, grocery store, mercantile and hardware store.

In addition to the mill itself, the company funded construction of a four-room brick schoolhouse in 1920. In 1937, it sold its industrial steam-generated electrical plant to Appalachian Power and used the money from that deal to build the Fieldale Community Center, below, which is still open. Swimming pools and basketball courts came later.

Fieldcrest Mills, River Road, Fieldale

In Martinsville, William Pannill founded the Pannill Knitting Company in 1925 to produce inexpensive long underwear. Pannill had worked at a cotton-spinning mill in Mayodan, North Carolina, but most of the nation's textile manufacturing at that time was done in the Northeast. So, Pannill packed his bags and moved north, getting a job as a janitor at a plant in Utica, New York.

His real motivation, however, was research.

"Mr. Pannill went up to New York and learned what it took to make textiles," A.C. Wilson said. "He would take notes and make detailed observations on everything that went into it."

When the time was right, he traveled south again and opened his own business in Martinsville, at the age of 44.

In the 1930s, a new product hit the market when New England textile mills began producing fleece-lined sweatshirts, and Pannill picked up on the idea.

The Pannill Knitting Co. building on Cleveland Street just off Market Street, in 1938 (left) and 2019 (below).
Photo at left in public domain

Courtesy of Harvest Foundation

Another view of the Pannill Knitting Co. plant, c. 1928.

In 1937, Pannill put his son-in-law, E.A. Sale, in charge of the sweatshirt operation and spun off a separate company called Sale Knitting. (Another son-in-law, Frank Lacy, would start Lacy Manufacturing five years later.) A 30,000-square-foot plant was built to house the Sale operations, and 50 employees were hired to produce sweatshirts in four colors: white, silver gray, gunmetal and ecru — a light beige.

Sale retired in 1953 and turned the company over to yet another Pannill son-in-law, William Franck, with the Henry J. Tully Corp. buying a majority interest. Four years later, the company moved into a huge structure at Franklin Street and Commonwealth Boulevard, already a symbol of the area's economic shift from tobacco to textiles. It had been built in 1896 by Rucker & Whitten Chewing Tobacco, but by the 1920s, it had become home to Martinsville Cotton.

More recently, it's been converted into a mixed-use complex known as the Commonwealth Centre.

The Lester Group bought the building in 2002 and added the distinctive clock tower over the front entrance.

Commonwealth Centre, 300 Franklin Street

Courtesy of Harvest Foundation

The same building during its incarnation as Martinsville Cotton.

In 1971, Sale Knitting became Tully Corporation — which changed its name to Tultex five years later — and Martinsville eventually became the "Sweatshirt Capital of the World," producing more of that particular garment than anywhere else.

Far more.

Until the early 1990s, five major textile mills in town churned out three-quarters of the sweatshirts made on the planet. (The bubble burst when it became cheaper to produce such products overseas, and companies either moved their factories abroad or gave up the ghost entirely.)

But Martinsville made more than sweatshirts. It made nylons, too.

In 1941, DuPont built a factory along the Smith River (seen in the postcard above) to produce nylon filament for hosiery. The material was still relatively new at the time: The process for creating it had been perfected just six years earlier, and DuPont already had a plant in Delaware. But the Martinsville plant could churn out more than twice as much nylon as the Delaware operation. When it opened, customer No. 1 was First Lady Eleanor Roosevelt, for whom its first pair of nylon stockings was produced in early November.

Barely a month later, Roosevelt's husband — President Franklin Roosevelt — took to the radio airwaves and announced that the Japanese had bombed Pearl Harbor, Hawaii. Before long, the plant took on a whole new mission: Instead of making hosiery, it turned its entire attention to creating nylon for parachutes and other war materials.

"It wasn't inconceivable that we would have been on the list" of places Hitler and the Nazis might have targeted, "because we made all the nylon for the paratroopers," said Dean Johnston, who grew up in Martinsville.

After the war ended, the 550-acre plant prospered. DuPont doubled its capacity and crowed that its two plants together could make 360 million pairs of nylon stockings in a year: enough for each woman in the United States to own 11 pairs. In the 1960s, the plant employed more than 4,600 workers.

How big a deal was the DuPont plant to Martinsville?

Just take a trip down to the area of town where the plant was located, along the Smith River not far from the Smith River Bridge over Route 220. The last stoplight before you get to the bridge, traveling south, is DuPont Road, which heads out to the plant. Much of the factory complex is now demolished, and it's closed to the public, but some of it is still visible. A rail line that fed the plant lies overgrown to the northeast, and the remnants of the DuPont sign can still be seen at the entrance.

Just up the hill from the crossing pictured above is the expansive mansion known as Lynwood House, which DuPont made available to its managers as living quarters — and which is named for the first manager to have resided there.

Lynwood House, 590 DuPont Road

In 1976, the property was occupied by the Piedmont Arts Association, which moved to the former Schottland Estate on Starling Avenue after the Schottland family donated that building in 1981. These days the pastor of Wellspring Fellowship lives at the home, and the congregation worships in an adjacent building.

DuPont also built an entire country club for its employees within view of the plant. The Lynwood Golf and Country Club opened in 1947 as a nine-hole course. Nine more holes were added in the 1970s, and around that time, the club opened its membership to those not on the DuPont payroll. Dues were $7.40 in 1964 and $112 a month in 2012, when the country club closed. In addition to a 6,000-yard, par-71 golf course, the club had a clubhouse, swimming pool, tennis courts and other recreational facilities.

"I spent lots of time at Lynwood over years," said Stephen Mark Rainey, who also taught drawing and painting at Lynwood House when it was the Piedmont Arts Center. "Learned to swim at the pool there. Played golf. Went to dances at the clubhouse in my 20s. I so hate it's gone."

What's left of the DuPont plant, with the sign support at the entryway (top).

The country club closed in early 2012, after members voted to cease operations so the 189-acre property could be sold to a private company that was interested in developing it as an industrial site. The DuPont factory itself had been closed for 14 years at that point. But more than a year after the club shut down, the deal that had been in the works fell apart. It was too late to reopen Lynwood at that point, so the area was left without both a golf course and an industrial occupant.

By 2019, the clubhouse had been torn down, the pool had been filled in, and the tennis courts were overgrown with weeds. Cart paths were barely visible beneath the overgrown brush. On one of them was stenciled, in faded letters, "SCATTER," instructing cart drivers not to create ruts in the landscaping by driving repeatedly over the same section of turf.

Courtesy of Hagley Museum and Library
The DuPont plant, with Smith River in the background, is seen from the air in this 1950s photo.

The jobs DuPont had brought to the city had scattered by then, too, as had those at Tultex and many other local manufacturers, most of them having been shipped overseas during the free-trade movement. In 1984, Tultex employed 8,000 people. Fifteen years later, it declared bankruptcy, and what was left of the company relocated to China.

The DuPont plant had closed just a year earlier, its payroll having withered to just 400, less than one-tenth of what it had been in the plant's heyday. Two years before that, the Sara Lee sewing factory had shut down.

Up until the 1990s, Martinsville was "a booming place," said Dean Johnston, a Martinsville High graduate who works as branch manager for Stifel, Nicolaus & Company on Main Street. "I think, at one point, we had more millionaires per capita than any other town on the East Coast. The names on the sides of the buildings, those people lived here. The Hookers and the Bassetts, they lived here."

Johnston said the North American Free Trade Agreement in 1994 had the same effect on Martinsville that Hurricane Katrina had on New Orleans: Nothing would ever be the same again. Generations of residents had worked at the nylon, textile and furniture plants after their forebears made the transition from an agriculture-based economy. Tobacco. Cotton.

When all those jobs left Martinsville, "you didn't hurt the people who owned the factory," Johnston said. "They'd already made their money. You hurt the people who worked in the factories. Grandma had worked at the textile plant. Mom had worked at the textile plant. Daughter was destined to work at the textile plant." When the plant shut down, Johnston asked, "where do you go?"

"Walmart learned that you could make sweatshirts in Honduras a whole lot cheaper than you could in Martinsville."

Nearly a decade after Tultex closed, Martinsville still had an unemployment rate of 22 percent. It had dipped to 15 percent by 2014, still nearly three times the national average. But by 2018, things had begun to turn around, with the city's jobless rate dipping to barely 5 percent, and Henry County's figure under 4 percent.

The transition continues, and Martinsville looks to a new future, what Johnston calls "a Phoenix type of moment," as a city with a reasonable cost of living, plenty of natural beauty and, increasingly, more to offer in terms of entertainment and culture than many might realize.

"I get emotional about the town," said Charles Roark, owner of Hollywood Cinemas. "I like little towns. I think the thing that we take for granted is we never have a traffic jam. You just get in your car, and you're home. And you know everybody. It's just fun. It's fun to know all these characters."

Church Street near Walnut

Retail

Uptown is to Martinsville what downtown is to many other cities:

The place everything started.

The heart of it all.

A lot has changed over the years, as it tends to do with city centers. Retailers have set up shop, moved to new locations, and shut down. The best location, in the early years, were Jones, Franklin and Main streets, which formed three sides of the courthouse square.

From there, businesses migrated south to Church Street and west along both Church and Main. An African-American business district sprang up a block to the north on Fayette Street and then spread westward, in the opposite direction.

The map below, produced by Sanborn Fire Insurance, shows what Martinsville looked like in 1891, with most businesses clustered around the square — and a lot of empty spaces still to be filled in.

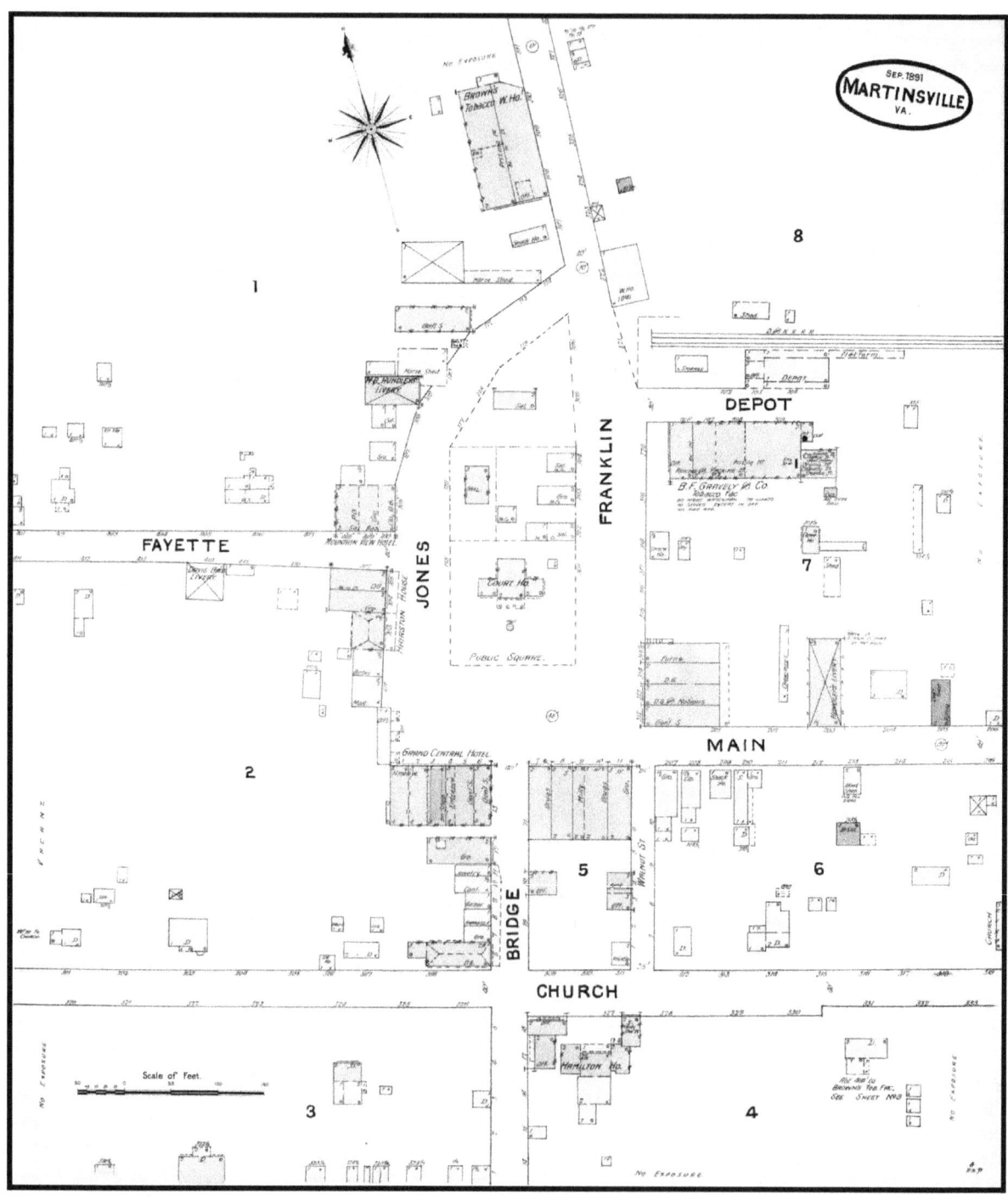

Martinsville Hotel Fayette and Jones

The businesses on the map aren't mentioned by name, but by type: There are a couple of drugstores and a couple of barbers. There's a bank, along with a few general stores, a jeweler, a millinery, two hotels and maybe half a dozen grocers.

Both hotels were near lots where others were built in later years: The Hamilton Hotel stood where the later Jefferson Hotel would be built around 1927 (an interesting contrast, considering the rivalry between the two early American leaders), and the Mountain View Hotel on Fayette would give way to the Martinsville Hotel about the same time.

Since the map predated the automobile, it's no surprise to find two livery stables and a horse shed, along with a harness shop, among the businesses represented.

Most prominent on the map is the B.F. Gravely & Co. tobacco factory, across from the train station. The map notes that the factory had "no night watchman, no lights, no stoves except in the office and no fire" equipment. What might have been a saloon (abbreviated on the map as "Sal.") stands conveniently near the courthouse and jail on Franklin Street.

Courtesy of Bassett Historical Center

You can see a picture of what the central square looked like during the period above.

Few businesses on the square survived deep into the 20th century, but one of them was Kearfott's Drug. The building at Bridge and Main, facing the courthouse, was built in 1891 — the same year that saw the construction of People's National Bank one block down at Main and Walnut. First National Bank, next door to Kearfott's, would be built in 1893 as Farmers Bank. (It became First National in 1904.)

As mentioned earlier, C.P. Kearfott came to Martinsville on the first passenger train to arrive at the station from Danville, and he promptly founded a pharmacy on the courthouse square. He also had ties to People's Bank, where he served as president for a number of years, and was a longtime member of the Virginia Pharmacy Board.

One of the most interesting facts about Kearfott, though, is that he was the first person in Martinsville to install a telephone, setting one of the newfangled devices up in the rear of his store. From there, a line to Ridgeway was established, funded by two businessmen in that town several miles to the south.

Kearfott Drugs was sold to Bud Shelton's Pharmacy in 1961. Although the First National Bank Building next door looks much the way it has for decades, Kearfott's has changed markedly over the years, covering up its original front (at right) with an orange-and-white mid-20th century modern façade that's reminiscent of a 50/50 ice cream bar. The contrast is apparent in these two photos, the one at top taken by the author in 2019, and the earlier, undated shot inset at lower right provided by the Bassett Historical Center.

Another early business on the courthouse square was Globman's, Martinsville's most notable homegrown department store, which was founded in 1915 by Abe Globman. Like

Kearfott, Globman arrived in Martinsville via the Danville & Western rail line, and set up shop in a 2,000-square-foot store.

Two decades later, that space had grown to 13,000 square feet in a three-story building on the square. The building had display windows not just on the lower floor, but on the second floor, too, and an early photo shows mannequins facing Franklin Street from that second story.

It was the place to be.

"All the commerce was done in downtown," said A.C. Wilson. "People came in from the country on Saturday, and it was alive with activity. People went there to do business and socialize. Everything centered around that, particularly in the late '20s and '30s. It was just a thriving new place to be. Banking was hot. My father came in the late '20s, and at least three of his Roanoke College roommates came to Martinsville for jobs."

*Globman's I
30 Franklin Street*

But in 1950, Globman's moved away from the courthouse square into an even larger space on Church Street: 54,000 square feet, to be exact. The old building became Shumate and Jessie Furniture and, later, the New College Institute's King Hall. At some point, those second-story display windows were filled in by cubes of opaque glass.

Globman's also expanded to other Virginia locations. A store in Galax was up and running in 1929. When the era of the indoor, air-conditioned shopping center arrived, Globman's opened 35,000-square-foot stores in the Eden Mall (1980) and Danville's Piedmont Mall — now the Danville Mall (1985). In Martinsville, however, the company resisted the urge to follow stores like Penney's and Belk to the new Liberty Fair Mall and remained uptown until it closed all its stores in 1991.

That uptown store had expanded to 90,000 square feet in 1961, with an additional 30,000 square feet in the same building dedicated to other businesses: Woolworth's took up the bulk of the space at 21,000 square feet, with the remainder going to Wampler's Drug Store and the Music Bar, which faced Main Street. Touting itself as "Martinsville's Complete Music Store," the Music Bar sold AM-FM radios, televisions, records (78, 45 and 33⅓ rpm), along with "all musical instruments and accessories."

Woolworth's like Globman's, had moved to its location from the city center, farther west on Church Street in a space it yielded to McCollum Ferrell Shoes. The new and old Woolworth locations are seen below.

Globman's II, 115 East Church

Another store that started out on the courthouse square stayed there throughout its history in Martinsville.

Mick-or-Mack had a grocery store on Jones Street, fronting the square by the 1930s, when the Roanoke-based chain was in the midst of a growth spurt despite the Great Depression.

The chain had opened its first store in 1927 and was one of the main early competitors for Kroger, which also had a Martinsville store in the '30s, next to the Rives Theatre. Unlike Kroger, however — which maintains a presence in Martinsville today — Mick-or-Mack didn't last ... at least not locally.

It had 43 stores in 38 Virginia towns by 1931, and the chain reached its zenith in the next decade with 60 stores.

MARTINSVILLE MEMORIES

Mick-or-Mack had a store in Martinsville by 1937, and it was still there 17 years later, selling "quality meats" and "fancy groceries." The chain touted its "cash talks" slogan and promoted itself as "the store that gives S&H stamps." When the stamps went out of vogue in the 1970s, however, the Mick-or-Mack chain suffered, contracting to just 13 stores by the mid-1980s.

Mick-or-Mack 41 Jones Street

Uptown Martinsville saw a number of other stores come and go over the years. McCollum Ferrell was "The Name for Fine Shoes in Martinsville," but it wasn't the only shoe store in town. Down the street at 41 Church was York's Fine Footwear, "Martinsville's Fashion Shoe Store."

C.W. Holt & Company, on the northeast corner of Bridge and Church, was the "House of Quality." The HOLT sign in bold lettering still stands out at the intersection. Morton's Men's Shop offered "Men's Wear for Anywhere" at 9 Church Street, and the Glamor Shop on Walnut invited customers to "Go Glamor, Dress Well, Save Money."

A number of jewelers also plied their wares.

Lloyd's on Church competed for business with Byrd's on Bridge. Kingoff's, which also had a store in Danville, promoted itself as "Martinsville's Leading Jewelers," while the Jewel Box on Church was "Your Friendly Credit Jewelers." Then, there was Rimmer's, founded in 1922 on Walnut Street. It later moved to 117 Main, where its sign remained visible — if partly hidden by tree branches — at its former location in 2019.

The neon Rimmer's sign still hangs above its former store on Martinsville's Main Street, left, and fancy green-and-white tile remains in the entryway of Kingoff's closed Danville store, below.

MARTINSVILLE MEMORIES

Courtesy of Martinsville-Henry County Historical Society

Uptown Martinsville looking west along Church (left) and Main streets in the 1950s. The new Globman's is toward the bottom near the center, across from First Baptist Church, with First Presbyterian just west of Globman's. The Henry Hotel and Chief Tassel Buildings stand across from one another, just west of First Baptist. Abe Globman bought both First Baptist and First Presbyterian, which built new sanctuaries, on Starling and Patrick Henry avenues, respectively. First Presbyterian was razed to make way for a new Woolworth attached to Globman's. The old First Baptist site is now a parking lot.

Courtesy Martinsville-Henry County Historical Society

Uptown from a different vantage point in the 1960s, looking roughly southeast, with Liberty and Franklin streets converging in the "Y" at the lower left. The prominent parking lot in the center is off Fayette Street, with Main Street one block up in the photo. At the upper left, First Presbyterian and First Baptist have been demolished, with the new Woolworth, which included Wampler's, in place. At left, looking up Franklin toward Main (author photo).

MARTINSVILLE MEMORIES

Photo above courtesy of Harvest Foundation

An early postcard view of the courthouse square and a photo of Church Street (looking west from near Broad Street) in the 1950s shows how the retail center of uptown shifted. Notice that Astor Café, top right, has moved to Church Street.

Globman's had competition downtown, too. United Department Store — the "Friendly Store of Values" — operated out of a space on Walnut Street in the ground floor of the People's Bank building. J.C. Penney arrived in 1928 and was a major competitor before it fled for the new Patrick Henry Mall in 1965, as was Montgomery Ward, which set up shop around 1930. That same year, Leggett's opened in a 7,000-square-foot rented space downtown, moving to 23 East Church Street five years later.

The Leggett's chain had an interesting history, dating back to 1888 when William Henry Belk started a bargain store in Monroe, North Carolina. Three years later, he took on his brother John as a partner, and John had connections with the Leggett family. In 1920, his nephew by marriage, Will Leggett, teamed up with the Belks to open a store in Burlington, North Carolina, while brother Fred Leggett started a store under the Belk-Leggett brand name in Danville, a half-hour from Martinsville.

MARTINSVILLE MEMORIES

The two branches of the family — and the business — went their separate ways in 1927, when they agreed that the Leggett brothers would own 80 percent of the new stores from then on, while the Belks would own the other 20 percent. When it came time to open a store in Martinsville, the Leggetts got the nod, and the nameplate.

That store quickly outgrew its original location and, five years later, made arrangements for a move to a new building on Church Street that was three times the size of its original space. It let its lease expire in preparation for the move. Unfortunately, the new building wasn't ready in time, and the store had to find someplace to store its merchandise in the interim.

That "someplace" turned out to be a farmer's warehouse, where the owner had housed his horses. Leggett's hastily removed the horses, swept the floors (thoroughly, one would hope) and provided lighting by setting fires in 50-gallon oil drums. The arrangement lasted for six weeks, and even proved to be a boon for business as customers showed up just to see what a department store in a horse stable might look like.

After the new store finally opened, even it didn't provide enough room, so Leggett's added an 8,000-square-foot bargain store at 33 Church Street 14 years later. It installed the city's first escalator in 1948 and modernized the building a couple of times, but space constraints eventually caught up with the store again.

Flash forward to 1966, more than a decade after Globman's moved to the eastern edge of uptown on Church Street. That's when Leggett's decided to follow suit, opening a 50,000-square-foot store (below) on a slope just down the block. You could enter the building from the main floor off Church Street or from the lower floor via the rear parking lot, which had room for 114 cars.

STEPHEN H. PROVOST

Montgomery Ward
20 East Church

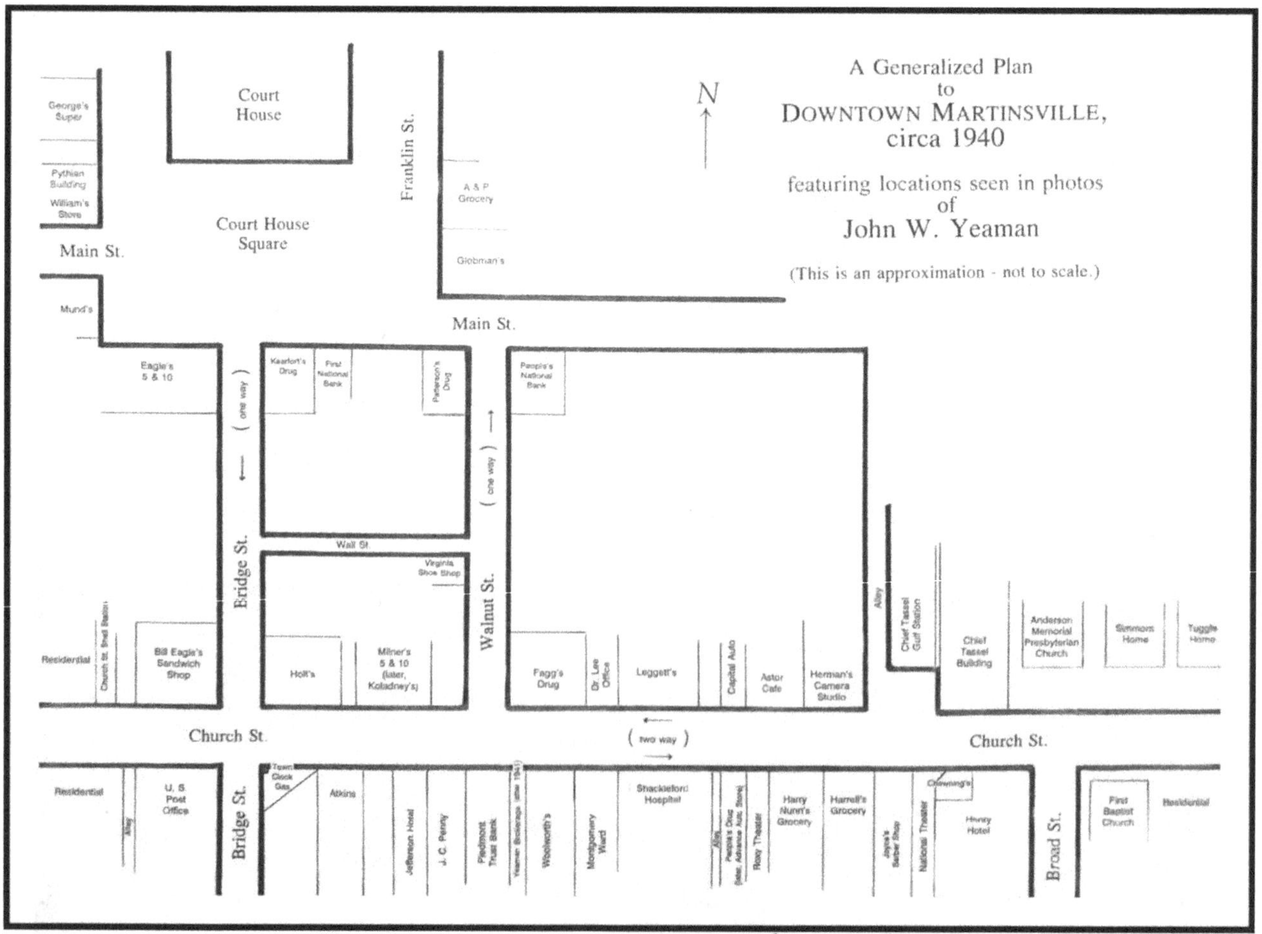

Courtesy of Martinsville-Henry County Historical Society

Courtesy of Bassett Historical Center

Two early postcard views of Church Street in Uptown Martinsville.

In 1996, things came full circle for Leggett's. Despite the earlier agreement, Belk had outgrown its former partner, having mushroomed into a chain with hundreds of locations. Leggett's, with 40 stores, was rumored to be exploring a merger with Dillard's when Belk stepped forward and bought a controlling stake in the company. Eventually, the Leggett name was retired, and the Belk name was applied to all former Leggett's stores.

As of 2019, Belk operated the city's only remaining major department store, at the reconfigured Liberty Hill Mall, now known as the Village of Martinsville.

Liberty Fair was a huge blow to uptown, but it wasn't the first one to be struck.

"A big fire came along in the '50s and wiped out some major buildings," A.C. Wilson recalled. "Bassett came along, and Fieldale, and all that diluted downtown a little. Shopping centers came along, and highways got better, so people started going to Danville and Greensboro to shop."

J.C. Penney closed its uptown shop on Christmas Eve 1965 and opened a new store in the city's first suburban shopping center, the Patrick Henry Mall, on Church and Brookdale streets. In *The Martinsville Bulletin*, Manager John Tadlock described the new store as a near-total break from the past, resembling its predecessor only in "name and reputation."

The new store had a new logo, replacing an antique octagonal sign that had been on the front of the uptown store since it opened in 1928. The old Penney store had employed 16 people, but there were more than 200 on the payroll at the new location, which covered 60,000 square feet — "more than 10 times as much space as we had at our old downtown store," Tadlock said.

The new store also had an auto center, something the old location lacked.

And it wasn't alone. Roses served as a second anchor for the new shopping center, at the rear of the mall, which also featured a People's Drug Store as a major tenant. Those were just two of 18 shops at the center, which also welcomed Music Bar from behind Globman's.

MARTINSVILLE MEMORIES

The Patrick Henry Mall, with the Penney's building at right and the Roses building at the rear.

Full roster of businesses at the new mall

Colonial Stores
Country Cobbler
Fast Service Cleaners
Glidden
Happy House Shop
J.C. Penney
J.C. Penney Auto Center
Marilyn's Shoes
Merle Norman Cosmetics
Music Bar
Patrick Henry Optical
Peoples Drug Store
Piedmont Trust Bank
Roses
Sportsman Barber Shop
Style City Beauty Salon
Singer
Three Sisters

The Patrick Henry was an outdoor mall, sort of a hybrid between your typical strip mall and a major outdoor shopping center. Like the former, it was arranged in an L shape around a parking lot — though that lot was far larger than those at most strip malls. Also like strip malls, it had a grocery store (Colonial) and a drugstore (People's), along with smaller neighborhood businesses such as a barber, dry cleaner and beauty salon.

On the other hand, it resembled a major mall in that it had an outdoor concourse in the back, complete with planters, that offered the feel of a stroll down a city street — without the traffic. Penney's, a shoe store, and a cosmetics shop added to the feel of a more substantial mall. Even today, there's some of that mix, thanks to stores like Ariel's Apparel, a women's clothier that moved into the center back in 1980 — and was still in business nearly four decades later.

When it opened, Patrick Henry Mall must have seemed like a death knell to downtown, although Globman's and Leggett's stayed put in their stores, roughly across from and catty-corner to each other on Church Street.

The Central concourse at the Patrick Henry Mall, facing the now-vacant Roses store (above), and the J.C. Penney building (right), which was occupied by a discount retailer as of 2019.

MARTINSVILLE MEMORIES

The Druid Hills Centre in 2019.

The Patrick Henry wasn't the only — or even the first — regional mall to appear in the Martinsville area during the period. Around 1960, at least two suburban hubs began to form: one in Collinsville, north of town, and the other at the south end in the Druid Hills-Forest Park area.

The Druid Hills Shopping Center on Spruce Street at Parkview, opened in the 1959 and fashioned itself as a sort of miniature suburban downtown. The architecture all followed the same Colonial-style theme, featuring red brick, white wooden gables and cupolas, with a few columns thrown in here and there for good measure. That wasn't just true of the shopping center, but also of nearby buildings in the area, such as the service station across the street and the post office next door.

Kroger was the main anchor and first tenant, later to be joined by such businesses as First National Bank, Druid Hills Drugstore and High's Ice Cream Parlor.

"Martinsville's friendliest super market" bragged that the center was "easy to reach from all over town." At the time, parts of Spruce Street and Brookdale Avenue were known as Old Danville Road, as seen on the map on the next page, from a Kroger ad.

"This is the only store of similar architecture in the Kroger chain, and we are extremely proud that it was erected here in Virginia," Paxton Judge, the company's vice president, told *The Staunton News-Leader* in announcing the store. "It was especially designed to blend with the beauty of residences in the area."

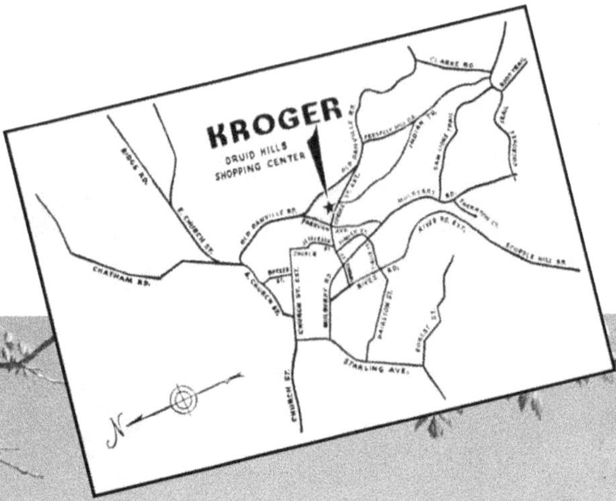

The Kroger at Druid Hills, above checked in at 13,500 square feet and featured a design that matched other buildings in the area. A Marathon gas station across the street, at right, also followed the Colonial theme.

The new shopping center served an area that had been developing since the late 1920s. Rives S. Brown and his sister Lucy had inherited a nearly 2,000-acre tract of land called Lanier Farm from their adoptive father, Henry Clay Lester. It had started off as the property of Patrick Henry, and the famed patriot had sold it to David Lanier. It was, as the name suggests, Lanier's farm, and it was used for that purpose until 1922.

Rives served as the farm superintendent, but Lester — who died in 1913 — had left the farm to both of them.

The shared inheritance got complicated when Lucy died, and her share of the farm passed to her husband, Morton Hundley. When

Courtesy of James Coleman

Rives S. Brown Sr., right, with his sister Lucy. In the background are ears of corn, which were grown on Lanier Farm.

he, in turn, died after remarrying, his new wife, Kate Black, gained title to half the farm.

"All of a sudden, he's got Kate Black as his partner, and he had to buy her out," explained James Coleman, who now runs the company the elder Rives Brown started. "I think he paid her $100,000, which at that time was a lot of money, and it kind of strapped him."

Not that Black would need the money. In 1933, she wed John Phillips, the son of oilman Frank Phillips — the founder of Phillips Petroleum/Phillips 66. But even though Rives Brown Sr. had to shell out six figures to gain full control of the farm, it turned out to be worth the investment.

Brown founded his real estate company in 1928 and, that same year, built the Chief Tassel Building on Church Street, across from the Henry Hotel. At the time they were

Rives S. Brown Sr. built the Chief Tassel Building, named for Overhill Cherokee Chief Old Tassel, or Corntassel, for whom Corn Tassel Road in Brown's Druid Hills development is also named.

built, the two four-story buildings served as a sort of eastern entrance to the commercial heart of the city, with a number of churches (naturally) situated to the east of them along Church Street.

But Brown's big project was Lanier Farm, which he saw as a place to develop homes.

His early plans involved just two roads: Mulberry Road, which was called Highland Ridge on the earliest blueprints, and Parkview Avenue. But he didn't start planning for a full-fledged new development until 1938.

The location turned out to be perfect. Three years later, DuPont built a new plant in Martinsville. The factory would need workers, and those workers would need housing. Fortuitously, the plant was near the southern edge of town — and so was the Lanier Farm.

"It all worked in his favor," Coleman said. "The development, DuPont coming here, the whole nine yards."

When Brown decided to build a full-fledged development beyond just Mulberry Road, he realized he would need help. So he enlisted the services of E.S. Draper, a landscape architect who came up with the overall design for the area to be called Forest Park. Draper also created the Charlotte neighborhood of Myers Park and was the first to design a residential suburb that included a golf course (in the Farmington Community near Charlottesville, Virginia). In his career, he designed more than 340 plans for subdivisions, resorts, estates and college campuses, and also served as director of land planning and housing for the Tennessee Valley Authority.

The centerpiece of Forest Park would be a manmade lake, Lake Lanier, where residents could picnic, paddle canoes or take a leisurely stroll.

As in Charlottesville, there would be a golf course, too: Forest Park Country Club. And the housing would complement the natural terrain of hills and valleys, with homes on large lots and the forested land preserved behind them.

"There were bridle trails, because a lot of the people on Mulberry had horses," Coleman said. "And there were pathways all going to the lake. All that was master-planned. With a lot of developments, you go in and it just happened: It's a hodgepodge or piecemeal. Not many areas go in that are master-planned, especially in a small city."

Stephen Mark Rainey's father was one of the DuPont employees who wound up buying a home in the development. Rainey grew up in a home on Indian Trail, across from a dense thicket of tall trees.

"It is a beautiful location," he said. "Used to play in the woods there all the time, and I still love to walk around in there. There's what appears to be a roadbed that I suspect goes back to when all that was farmland.

"When I was a kid, there was still an old horse barn down by the creek — 'Frankie's barn,' it was called, because the horse was named Frankie. Apparently, Frankie fell into the creek and broke his legs, so he had to be put down. Local legend has it that, on certain nights, you can hear Frankie crying out in pain. Alas, in almost 60 years, I've never heard such a thing."

The Druid Hills retail center, which went in next to Forest Park, was master-planned, too. By the time it was built, Rives S. Brown Jr. was in charge of the company, his father having passed away in 1951.

The name Druid Hills, however, came from not from either Brown, but from Draper, the landscape architect: "There was a Druid Hills in Atlanta, Georgia, and the same gentleman who did that development, he did this one here," Coleman explained. "I don't know which one was first."

Kroger was a natural choice to anchor the new regional shopping center Brown had planned, because the elder Brown had built a Kroger store in the '30s next to his Rives Theatre (more on this in the next chapter). The only thing the new center didn't have was a department store. Stores like Penney's and Leggett's and Globman's would remain downtown for now.

But it was only a matter of time before that changed.

MARTINSVILLE MEMORIES

The old uptown Kroger at Church and Clay streets then and now (above, right), per James Coleman. Below, the Kroger at Druid Hills after it opened.

Top, bottom photos courtesy of James Coleman

Up the road, the Collinsville Shopping Center opened in 1962, anchored by Leggett's. For the store's grand opening, it offered free bus rides to and from downtown Martinsville, Fieldale, Stanleytown and Bassett. The era of suburban shopping had begun.

Winn-Dixie added its third area supermarket at the center, joining its established locations on Memorial Boulevard and on Fayette Street, near the city center. Other attractions at the new supersized strip mall included Wickline-Mann Drugs, an Eagle Stores 5&10 variety shop, Western Auto, Arcade Fashions — women's and girls' wear — and Shoe Center (with "shoes for every member of the family).

The $800,000 center opened on 11½ acres, with enough parking for 400 cars.

As you can see by the roster of stores underneath the center's sign today (above), the mall has changed quite a bit since its heyday, with discount stores such as Family Dollar and Save a Lot having supplanted Leggett's and Winn-Dixie. The center's main anchor in 2019 was a Shewels Furniture Store.

Other regional and neighborhood shopping centers started popping up, as well, in the 1960s and '70s. One at Greensboro and Rives roads at the southern end of town featured a Kmart, Winn-Dixie and Revco Drug. That center was eventually razed, and the Kmart jumped over to the other side of Greensboro Road to join Food Lion before going out of business in 2016. Rural King moved into that spot two years later. (Winn-Dixie stores in Martinsville became Food Lions when Winn-Dixie pulled out of Virginia in 2005.)

Back in Collinsville, a quirky looking strip mall climbed the hill on the east side of the street, with the storefronts looking like a row of dominoes placed sideways.

It was called the Holiday Shopping Center.

Various other strip malls appeared, including several along Memorial Boulevard, which quickly became the main retail option to the city center — until, that is, Liberty Fair came along.

J.C. Penney, which had defected from its uptown store to the Patrick Henry Mall in 1965, jumped ship yet again when Liberty Fair became the city's first indoor shopping center in 1989. Leggett's moved in, too, along with a new Sears store and that rising behemoth of retailing, Walmart, giving the mall four major anchors. Other original tenants included RadioShack and The Pierced Ear.

But Liberty Fair came along toward the end of the big shopping mall boom, which had begun in the 1970s, and in just a few short years, it began to seem almost as outdated as the old Patrick Henry.

The first cracks started to show in 1997, when Walmart abandoned the center for a standalone store down the road, at the west end of Commonwealth Boulevard. OfficeMax, Kroger and Goody's took its place.

Two years later, the Penney's was downgraded to an outlet store, but the mall hung in there until things began to slip in 2012. The big blow was Sears' decision to pull out,

Courtesy of Alison M.
Jo-Ann Fabrics and a jewelry store offering "Cash for Gold" were among the tenants at the enclosed Liberty Fair Mall before it was converted into an outdoor "power center."

followed in 2013 by the loss of RadioShack, The Pierced Ear and Chick-fil-A (which also built a standalone store nearby). At this point, only one of the four anchors was left: Leggett's, which by this time had been rebranded as Belk. Stores began to flee the anchorless areas of the mall and cluster around the entrance to Belk.

Trees growing in the mall's corridors were removed after an arborist noted they were becoming overgrown. Potted plants replaced them, giving customers a clearer line of sight to notice other retailers in the mall. Those that remained, that is. As the holiday shopping season got under way in 2012, no fewer than dozen storefronts stood vacant in the mall. Sears was moving out, and the mall owners said they'd found no serious interest in a replacement.

As vacancies piled up along increasingly lonely corridors, the property owners ultimately decided to scrap the indoor mall concept entirely. Tearing down the J.C. Penney building, they rebuilt the mall as a power center: a glorified strip mall with Belk and Kroger as the main anchors, along with Marshall's — which had replaced Goody's — OfficeMax and a new Dunham Sports store.

Jo-Ann Fabrics, Rue 21 and GNC were among the stores that survived the transition. Those that didn't included Country Cookin', Hibbett Sports, Rack Room Shoes, and Bath & Body Works. At this point, the mall was renamed Village of Martinsville.

Leisure

In some communities, residents head to the movies or the bowling alley or the golf course in their spare time. They do that in Henry County, too, but whereas a cinema might seat a few hundred people, the main attraction in Martinsville can accommodate four or five times the population *of the city itself*.

Larger cities have big-league baseball or pro football teams that play in stadiums smaller than Martinsville Speedway, which can hold up to 65,000 people and hosts a pair of NASCAR stock-car races each year.

The track, just south of Martinsville in Ridgeway, actually predates NASCAR and is the only track still on the circuit from the National Association for Stock Car Racing's first season, 1948. It opened in September of the previous year as a half-mile dirt track, built for somewhere between $85,000 and $105,000, depending on the source.

Top photos by the author; bottom photo public domain

MARTINSVILLE MEMORIES

The Danville Bee said the new track boasted "the largest grandstand of any speedway in the South," with room for 20,000 people, adding that 10,000 were expected for opening day, September 7. Those numbers, however, may have been slightly exaggerated. According to the speedway's official site, only 750 seats were in place for that first day of racing, which was witnessed by a paying crowd of just over 6,000.

According to *The Bee*, 35 of the nation's top drivers had signed up to "risk their necks and cars" for a $2,000 purse. Three 12-lap qualifying heats were planned, to be followed by a 15-lap consolation race and a main feature covering 50 laps. Red Byron won the feature to claim the top prize of $500.

Byron would go on to become NASCAR's first Modified champion the following year, and its first Strictly Stock champion in 1949 — when he also won the 100-mile Virginia stock car championship in Martinsville. (The Strictly Stock title would later become known as the Winston Cup, Sprint Cup or Monster Energy Cup series, depending on the sponsor, beginning in 1971.)

The first NASCAR-sanctioned race was held at the track on Independence Day, 1948, with Pee Wee Martin of nearby Bassett placing second in the feature behind Fonty Flock — who had gotten into racing by delivering moonshine.

The speedway added 5,000 concrete seats to the West Grandstand in 1948, and the track was one of the first to host a live broadcast in '52 — five weeks behind Darlington Raceway in South Carolina. The track was paved midway through the 1955 season, and more seats were added in 1956, '57 (when the East Grandstand was built) and '60. Also in 1960, the track added the first air-conditioned press box on the NASCAR circuit.

Racing legend Richard Petty, born just an hour to the south in Level Cross, North Carolina, has started more races than anyone else at Martinsville, 67, also taking the checkered flag more than anyone else with 15 wins and adding 15 other top-five finishes. Jeff Gordon had the most top-10 finishes (38) as of 2019, and Darrell Waltrip had won the most poles, with eight.

NASCAR races have been held in Martinsville every fall since 1949 and each spring since 1950. The fall race was known as the Old Dominion 500 beginning in the mid-'50s, when the spring race was christened the Virginia 500, although both took on names to reflect shifting corporate sponsorships starting in the 1980s.

But why such a big speedway so close to such a small town?

Richard Petty, above, in 1973, has won more races at Martinsville than any other driver. At right, Red Byron's car. Byron won the first race ever held at the track.

Top photo Creative Commons, North Carolina State Archives
Bottom photo public domain

MARTINSVILLE MEMORIES

The answer lies in the fact that this small town was close to the heart of a very big business back in the 1920s. Not textiles. Not furniture.

Alcohol.

Fonty Flock wasn't the only driver who'd started off in the business of bootlegging (making deliveries on his bicycle as a young teen). A lot of others did, too. And even once they hit the tracks, some of them stayed involved ... because running alcohol for moonshiners paid better than racing did in the early days.

Virginia had a long history of promoting — and defying — efforts to outlaw alcohol. Prohibition took effect for the rest of the country at the tail end of 1920, but Virginia had voted to go "dry" four years earlier. Moonshiners started cranking up their stills, and the epicenter of their activity was rural land in Franklin County, which stood directly between Roanoke and Martinsville. FBI Director J. Edgar Hoover dubbed it "the wettest place on earth."

The moonshiners needed fast cars, and men who could drive them, if they were to outrun and outwit police and hijackers determined to foil their black-market business. These drivers were known as bootleggers, after the practice of hiding bottles of liquor in their boots.

Before Prohibition even took effect nationally, they were already perfecting their skills. Police quickly learned that they could identify a bootlegger by listening for the gurgling sound made by the liquor as the cars traveled bumpy country roads. So, the bootleggers developed "non-gurgling" cans and imported them by the boxcar-load. Over a four-year span, 600,000 of the five-gallon cans found their way into Franklin County.

Then, there were driving strategies that could be employed. A report in the *Richmond Times-Dispatch* dated July 19, 1920, remarked that drivers had resorted to "naval techniques" in their efforts to thwart officers on the highway: They were now forming convoys, employing a large car to delay officers so the speedier bootleg cars could get away.

"A recent adventure in Martinsville reveals this," the newspaper reported. "Officers on Wednesday night saw two suspicious cars headed for Patrick (County). They waylaid the cars a few miles beyond Martinsville, expecting the machines to return. They did, a small car with a heavy load being followed by a seven-passenger machine of powerful build.

Library of Congress
A police officer stands beside a bootlegger's crashed car, alongside boxes of moonshine jars, in November 1922.

"The little car went by like a flash, and when the officers put in chase, the heavier car maneuvered to keep the road (clear) and blocked all efforts of the Henry County officers to get by."

The attempted getaway failed, however, when the larger car pulled too wide around a curve, and the officers were able to shoot past it — foreshadowing a maneuver in which stock-car racers pass on the inside when a car ahead of them rides up high around a curve. Police shot at the fleeing bootleg car several times before it crashed into a ditch, and the stunned youth behind the wheel was taken into custody.

Reports such as this filled the pages of Virginia newspapers during the 1920s, with both sides claiming victories.

In one report from 1922, Martinsville police said they had seized 138 gallons of moonshine — including 52 following a chase in which an alleged bootlegger was shot and wounded while attempting to escape. Two men leapt from the fleeing car during the pursuit, and the third was trying to scale a fence when an officer grabbed him and shot him during a struggle. The man was hit under the arm, and taken to Shackelford Hospital on Church Street.

Thinking the man badly injured, police neglected to place a guard on his room. But his wounds turned out to be less serious than they had believed, he managed to make his escape.

Prohibition brought out all sorts of schemes and stories.

One man in Lynchburg posed as a bootlegger, picked up his customers' moonshine, collected $4,000 from their banks, then fled without making the agreed-upon deliveries. In another odd twist, doctors in 1922 were complaining they couldn't get medicinal whiskey from licensed pharmacists and were being forced to rely on bootleggers for their supply. And a provision in the law that allowed the state to confiscate and resell bootleggers' cars had an unintended consequence: After 30 cars were impounded in Martinsville, they were later resold at rock-bottom prices — cutting into the sales of private car dealers.

One thing needed to make moonshine is sugar, but buying large quantities of it could draw unwanted attention. Dean Johnston told one story of a moonshiner who sent 50 different people to the store to buy sugar in order to avoid detection. Of course, that didn't keep from tipping off authorities that a ridiculous amount of sugar was being sold at a single store.

Not that it helped law enforcement much.

During a four-year period in Franklin County, nearly 34 million pounds of sugar were sold. Since the county had a population of just 24,000 at the time, that worked out to just over 354 pounds of sugar each year for every single county resident during the period.

It was a similar story with yeast, another important ingredient in the process of making moonshine. Over that same span of four years, Franklin County imported more than 70,000 pounds of the stuff — 35 times the consumption in Richmond, which had nearly eight times the population.

Meanwhile, and bootleggers took to bribing underpaid police officers with "granny fees" to look the other way, not just in Franklin County, but in Henry, Patrick and Floyd counties, too.

With so many drivers in the business of bootlegging, there was always the chance that honest officers could get it wrong. And sometimes they did. In February of 1925, S.B. Gatewood was driving home with his family from a basketball game in Martinsville, when two officers shot out his tires — only to discover he wasn't carrying any liquor.

The men refused to give their names after Gatewood's car came to a halt, but he conducted his own personal investigation and discovered their identities. (He later told a reporter that they were "very nice about it" and offered to reimburse him out of their own pockets for the damage to his vehicle.)

On weekends, bootleggers would test their skills against one another on makeshift dirt tracks across the South — a practice that evolved into more formal races and, eventually, into the NASCAR circuit.

The first organized stock-car race took place in 1936 at Daytona, Florida, and in 1947, a former moonshine runner named Bill France brought together a group of drivers, mechanics and car owners to lay down a standardized set of rules. That marked the beginning of NASCAR. Red Byron, a former bootlegger, won the first NASCAR race ever held, in February 1948 at Daytona.

Locally, Horsepasture native Hubert Hensley, a mechanic and owner of Hensley Racing, was inducted into the Virginia Motorsports Hall of Fame in 2018. His nephew Jimmy Hensley had received the same honor in 2013.

Top NASCAR drivers from Martinsville area

	Starts	Wins	Top 10	Poles	Active
Buddy Arrington	560	0	103	0	1965-1988
Johnny Bryant, Bassett (modifieds)	19	1	2	0	1985-1992
Clay Campbell	16	0	0	0	2011-2014
Ted Canady, Collinsville	15	0	0	0	1956-1957
Fred Dove	47	0	12	0	1952-1955
Jeff Hensley, Ridgeway	90	0	24	0	1982-1985
Jimmy Hensley, Ridgeway	98	0	15	1	1972-1996
Coleman Lawrence	22	0	6	0	1951-1953
Otis Martin, Bassett	23	0	6	0	1949-1954
Clyde Minter	42	0	18	0	1949-1955

MARTINSVILLE MEMORIES

Martinsville Speedway

This page and the pages following show views from Martinsville Speedway.

MARTINSVILLE MEMORIES

Courtesy of Harvest Foundation

Bowling

Bowling was huge in the 1960s. The PBA (Pro Bowlers Association) Tour got rolling in 1958, and when *The Flintstones* debuted two years later, viewers got a chance to see Fred take aim at those prehistoric pins on a regular basis.

By the middle of the decade, there were some 12,000 bowling alleys (or centers) across the country, generating more than two-thirds of their business via league membership.

Sportlanes, at left, opened its doors in Collinsville amid this bowling boom, making its debut in 1962 in a converted Chrysler building on Route 220. An ad in *The Martinsville Bulletin* touted it as "locally owned and operated," in contrast to Druid Lanes, which had opened a year earlier.

According to the business, it was originally designed to provide a "country club" atmosphere, complete with "a wooden picket fence around it and a corral for the kids!"

Sportlanes was still going strong in the 21st century. The bowling center also includes a café and bar, featuring a wide selection of beers and karaoke on Thursday nights.

The Senior PBA Tour staged its South Regional tournament there in 2008. A year later, Jason Osgood came within one strike of a perfect 900 series, a feat accomplished just 12 times nationally over the previous 12 years. Osgood may have missed three-game perfection by a whisker, but his effort still set a local record of 300-278-300.

MARTINSVILLE MEMORIES

Sportlanes, however, wasn't the first bowling alley/center in Martinsville. That honor belongs to the Martinsville Bowling Center, which was housed in the nondescript brick building pictured above, just off the courthouse square.

Today, it's a barbershop and beauty salon. But when it was built around 1935, it served as a destination for Henry County bowlers. The game was a bit different back then, though. The Martinsville Bowling Center opened in an era before automatic pinsetters: Someone at the end of the lane had to collect and reposition the pins manually after each ball was rolled. It wasn't until the advent of automated pinspotters in the middle of the 20th century that the sport really took off.

The bowling craze it spawned, however, has largely died down. The leagues that drove so much business toward bowling alleys during their heyday are far fewer now. So are bowling centers themselves. As of 2007, the number was less than half what it was during the sport's peak in the 1960s, with fewer than 5,500 certified 10-pin bowling centers in operation.

Among those that called it quits was Druid Lanes, built for more than half a million dollars back in 1960. *The Bulletin* called it "the greatest outlay of money in the history of the city for recreational facilities." At more than 22,000 square feet, the 24-lane operation would include a kitchen, snack bar, meeting room and nursery. It would be operated by the American International Bowling Corporation, a New York-based company that already had alleys with 1,500 lanes in 20 cities nationwide.

Druid Lanes, 1051 Spruce Street

"They used to have great pizza there when I was a kid," Stephen Mark Rainey recalled. "And the lounge was called 'The 'alf Pint.' When my folks took me there to get pizza, I'd hear people enjoying themselves in there, and see men in business suits coming and going. I always wanted to go in, but Dad told me, 'That's the place for grown-ups.' So, I really, *really* wanted to go there. When I started going in as a teenager, it *was* fun. A nice little bar, though it went downhill in later years.

"In my senior year of high school, my friend Joe had picked up a tube of Super Glue.

It was when the stuff first came out, and he wanted to test it. So, being a wise ass, he super-glued a half-full glass of beer to the linoleum table in The 'alf Pint. (This would have been 1977.) Next time we went inside, we sat down at the same table, and there was a big, gouged-out ring where they'd had to rip that glass up. That table with the gouged ring was still stayed in there for 30 years — I sat there many, many times over that period."

Druid Lanes closed sometime in the 2010s, and the sign was taken down. But, as of 2019, you could still peek through the front windows and see old seats, a scoring pencil and even a pair of bowling shoes gathering dust near the front of the building.

Golf

In addition to the Lynwood Golf and Country Club, the Martinsville area featured — and still features — several courses for those interested in testing their skill on the links. Forest Park Country Club on Mulberry Road (in image below, c. 1960, courtesy of James Coleman) is a 6,624-yard, par-72 course in the Druid Hills area of Martinsville.

Chatmoss Country Club on Mount Olivet Road offers a par-72 course that covers 6,871 yards, while Beaver Hills Golf Club serves up a shorter layout (5,894 yards) at par 71. For those who prefer a par-3 layout, Horsepasture, seven miles west of town, offers a nine-hole executive course with a total par of 27, just off Route 58.

Movies

Rives Theatre, 215 East Church

Courtesy of Dean Johnston

The 652-seat Martin on Starling Avenue, at left. Below, an office building on Starling preserves a nearly identical street-facing design.

Above left photo W. Sasser, cinematreasures.org, Creative Commons license; author photo above.

Motion pictures in Martinsville dated back at least to 1915, when the Hamilton Theatre opened in front of the Hotel Hamilton. The city had 4,000 people then, a figure that would nearly double by the time of the Great Depression. The number of theaters would double, too.

The Roxy and National, two of Martinsville's earliest theaters, were just a few doors down from each other on Church Street. The Roxy had enough room for 505 people, with the National seating close to the same number, 494. The movies themselves were shown at the rear of the buildings, which were fronted by retail space. But that didn't stop the theaters from making a splash.

The Roxy and National beckoned theatergoers with lighted signs out front and luxurious lobbies. The Roxy even featured an indoor fountain and a sandwich shop. And, in 1930, the National touted itself as "The Temple of the Motion Picture," equipped with a Western Electric Sound System.

The Roxy continued to operate into the 1960s, but it and the National eventually closed when downtown theaters began giving way to suburban cinemas.

Still, the Rives, down the block, remained open. Uptown's first detached movie theater, it was built by Rives S. Brown — the same developer behind the Forest Park and Druid Hills neighborhoods (and whose name graces Rives Road). Brown and partner Bernard Depkin got into the theater business when they built the Rives for $50,000.

A 1941 ad for Charlie Chaplin in *The Great Dictator* at Martinsville's Roxy.

The first movie was screened at the Rives on October 9, 1935, and drew a crowd of 900 people for what *The Danville Bee* described as a "gala event."

"The guests were greeted by a group of Martinsville's most beautiful young ladies, and given a favor from the theatre owners," the newspaper reported. "The foyer was bedecked with floral blossoms of roses, chrysanthemums and palms."

The mayor appeared on a lighted stage to thank the crowd at 8 p.m. Then the lights dimmed, and theatergoers enjoyed a showing of *Red Salute*, an anti-communist comedy featuring Robert Young (*Father Knows Best*) and Barbara Stanwyck (*The Big Valley*). People from all over the area, from South Boston to Salem, from Ridgeway to Reidsville, and even from as far away as New York City, attended the opening night.

By the following year, however, the theater got in a bit of hot water when it tried to attract more patrons with what it called a "Bank Night." Prosecutors alleged that the theater was operating an illegal lottery by offering a cash prize to the winner of a drawing at the theater. The theater manager countered that the promotion was legal because participants didn't have to buy a ticket to win. Still, the theater voluntarily ended the contests a couple of months later.

Other promotions were less controversial. In 1962, Susan's Shoppe in the Druid Hills Shopping Center offered free children's passes to see *Lady and the Tramp* at the Rives with the purchase of $10 or more. That same year, pop stars Joey Dee and the Starlighters (who'd had a chart-topping hit with a song called *Peppermint Twist*) appeared at the theater in 1962 to promote a pair of recent movies they'd made: *Hey, Let's Twist* and *Two Tickets to Paris*. Admission was just $2 for the two-hour live show.

Originally constructed using concrete masonry, the Rives underwent a major renovation in the summer of 1964 that gave it a new front and marquee, an improved sound system augmented by acoustically treated ceilings and new, modern seats. It became the venue of choice for many local residents for a night out to watch a movie, or to sit in the parking lot while a holiday parade passed by.

The theater staff were helpful and friendly. After a Collinsville woman purchased a ticket to the show on a summer evening in 1967, she was dismayed to find she'd lost one of her contact lenses on the sidewalk out front. When she was unable to find it, the management gave her a refund ... which she used to watch the same movie the next night after her fiancé returned and, in a stroke of good fortune, found the lost lens.

In a news report on the incident, the woman thanked "a lot of nice people" who helped her look for the lens and said, when she finally got to see the film, that she "enjoyed it very much."

Police tape rings the Rives Theatre, and ashes litter the sidewalk on the morning after the fire that gutted the building.

Stephen Mark Rainey said that, of all the theaters in the area, "the Rives was where I spent the most time as a lad."

"Rarely did a weekend go by that I didn't attend one of the Saturday or Sunday matinees — always either at 1 p.m. or 3 p.m. — and I'd occasionally go to the regular evening shows as well, especially once I got my driver's license and could transport myself and whatever company I might be keeping at the time. A pudgy, white-haired gentleman named Tommy managed the theater, and he was a fixture there for more years than I can recount."

He recalled seeing movies from *The Wizard of Oz* to *The Planet of the Apes* to *The Poseidon Adventure* "in that dark, familiar auditorium."

"I believe it was in the 1980s that the theater was remodeled and divided into two auditoriums. At that point, it never seemed quite the same, yet it was still undeniably the Rives. A damn fun place to be."

In 2019, the Rives wasn't showing movies, but it did host live events ranging from concerts to open-mic nights — until a fire gutted the building on September 8.

Fire

Martinsville fire officials said the Rives Theatre looked like a total loss after a fire that started in the attic area of the building on the night of September 8, 2019. The photo above shows the building on the morning after the fire, which caved in the roof of the 10,000-square-foot structure, but didn't spread to any neighboring businesses.

Uptown has seen other fires over the years. A 1951 blaze caused $1 million in damage, destroying the Banner Warehouse on Franklin Street, where it started, along with the Henry County Furniture Co. and B.H. Townes buildings on Franklin. Also lost were the Brooks Machinery site and the third floor of the Lehman Knitting Mill on Depot Street.

Fifteen years earlier, in December 1936, a fireworks company had set up shop on the courthouse square in preparation for the New Year's holiday. But when a clerk set out to demonstrate a cap pistol, a spark landed in a pile of firecrackers, and soon two truckloads of fireworks were going off inside the building. Locals, hearing the bangs and pops, thought they were being invaded or a bank was being robbed. The building was flattened, but the only person hurt was the clerk, who sprained his ankle running away.

MARTINSVILLE MEMORIES

Top photo from an undated trade publication "Concrete Masonry for Better Buildings" produced by the Portland Cement Association. Used under a Creative Commons license. Bottom photo by author, taken less than a month before the fire.

The Martin Theatre was open by 1949 on Starling Avenue between Memorial and Market. With room for more than 600 patrons, it was the city's first truly suburban theater — but it wouldn't be the last.

Movie Town, with five screens, became Martinsville's first multiplex when it opened in 1984, and Hollywood Cinemas became the second in 2001. The latter features four 150-seat theaters and one with 50 seats that can double as an auditorium for televised events such as political debates. Charles Roark, who owns Hollywood Cinemas, also runs a TV station, WGSR, out of the building, which he built for $150,000.

The Hollywood video sign, top, overlooks the Walmart parking lot. Inside, above, are video games, novelty items and mannequins of various superheroes, including Wonder Woman (pictured), Deadpool, Batman and Iron Man. At left, the sign for Movie Town.

MARTINSVILLE MEMORIES

Then there were the drive-ins. The Family Drive-In Theater opened in 1948 with space for 300 cars off U.S. 220 at Bassett Forks north of Collinsville. But it closed its doors in 1973 to make room for a cloverleaf interchange with State Route 57 the following year.

In the 1970s, RC Theatres operated a pair of local drive-ins: the Martinsville and the Castle. The Martinsville Drive-In debuted on Joseph Martin Highway in 1948. Four years later, Jessie Carper — who also ran Castle Court Motel, a mile north of Martinsville on Route 220 — opened the similarly named Castle Drive-In at Florida and Wagoner in Collinsville. (RC bought the theater later on.)

The Castle Court Motel was air-conditioned and "completely modern," according to one of its postcards.

The Martinsville theater had room for 330 cars, and the Castle could accommodate 500.

Donna Vance of Ridgeway used to go to the Martinsville Drive-In. "I remember going to the movies there as a kid with family," she recalled. "We would lie on a quilt in the grass to watch the show and play during intermission. The concession stand had a low, flat roof, and sometimes Flatt and Scruggs or Bill Monroe would play old-timey mountain music."

Stephen Mark Rainey, a big fan of Godzilla movies, remembers a double bill in 1973 that presented an unpleasant quandary for the young monster-movie buff. The good news: *Destroy All Monsters*, featuring none other than Godzilla, was coming to the

Castle. The bad news: It was the *second* film on a double bill with *Yog, Monster from Space*.

"Rainey recalled that "while my parents didn't mind occasionally taking me and some friends to see monster movies, they inevitably ruled that the second feature came on too late for us to stay up."

"Well, I wanted to see *Destroy All Monsters* because it was a Godzilla movie; I knew nothing and cared nothing about Yog. Naturally, according to the published schedule, Yog was to be the first feature. So I called the drive-in, hoping to convince them to run *Destroy All Monsters* first. No way, they told me; the projector was set up to run Yog first, and that was that.

"Well, young Mark is distressed. So for a couple of evenings, I called the drive-in relentlessly, disguising my voice, even getting my best friend Frank to call them, hoping to persuade them to run *Destroy All Monsters* first. Each call was answered with the inevitable 'No way.'

"Well, come the weekend, my Dad takes us out there, we stop at the ticket booth, ask which show comes on first, and we're told '*Yog, Monster From Space*.' (The lady pronounced it like 'Yoga.') So Dad says, 'Sorry boys,' and figures we'll want to leave. But no; we put on the pressure and get him to drive us on in, just to see if maybe the ticket lady had made a mistake.

"Well, since we didn't pay, the manager comes to pay us a visit, and Dad tells him, 'We just figured we'd stay for a few minutes to see which movie came on first.' The manager bends down and gives Frank and me a very hard stare. 'You must be those youngsters who've been calling nonstop for the last two days.' We admit that we are. The manager sighs and says, 'Well, we've decided to run *Destroy All Monsters* first.' "

"You could hear us whoopin' and hollerin' over in the next county (which was actually just a stone's throw away). So it was a wonderful night for monsters."

The Castle stayed open for six years after that, but both it and the Martinsville Drive-In showed their final movies on the same night in 1979. The final bill was a triple-feature of *The Incredible Melting Man*, *The Incredible Two-Headed Transplant* and *The Thing With Two Heads*. There's an open field where the Castle used to be, and all that's left to remind residents of the Martinsville Drive-In's once-upon-a-time presence is the name of a street — Theatre Road — at the intersection where it once stood.

MARTINSVILLE MEMORIES

In their heyday, however, Martinsville drive-ins must have done a booming business, because in 1968, a fourth outdoor theater opened not too far from the Castle. The 220 Drive-In on Koehler Road, just off Business 220 in Collinsville, featured a 90-foot steel screen, an air-conditioned snack bar and stereo sound in the comfort of your car. It opened on Labor Day weekend, just in time for the new school year, with Clint Eastwood's *Hang'Em High*.

Right down the street from Sportlanes, the 220 gave teens what amounted to a one-stop date night destination. The drive-in, which had space for 460 cars, didn't just play movies, either. In 1970, it hosted the O'Kaysions — a North Carolina band that had recently had a hit with *Girl Watcher* — and the Drifters in a concert double bill.

But the 220 went the way of so many other outdoor theaters as the curtain fell on the era of the drive-in. It went out of business in 1987, going dark after a double-feature of *Dragnet* and *Crocodile Dundee*.

The next day, a 50-year flood hit the area, and the theater never reopened. In 2019, little more than a few bits of asphalt, the old ticket booth and two rusted light standards at the entrance remained as evidence that it had ever been there.

Liberty Heights Pool

Swimming

It can get hot in Henry County during the summer. The average temperature is 87 in July and 85 in August, and 90-90 days (temperature plus humidity) can make it feel like a sauna.

What's the best alternative to a sauna? A swimming pool, of course. And for many years, Martinsville had one. It wasn't just any pool, either, but a huge outdoor public pool called Liberty Heights.

From the outside, it looked like a football stadium. Inside, it was an oval pool with a circumference of 1,000 feet that could hold 2,000 — yes, two *thousand* — swimmers at one time.

The pool was the brainchild of G.T. Lester, whose Lester Lumber Company had been hit by several fires. In response, he built a 2 million-gallon concrete reservoir in 1920 on high ground (hence, the "Heights" name) and laid piping that ran downhill to his plant. Water was pumped from Jones Creek into the three-tier concrete structure, which Lester modeled after a spiderweb because it was "one of the strongest forces in nature."

Six years later, when the Kiwanis Club approached him for a contribution to build a new municipal pool, he offered to transform this reservoir into just that.

And so, he did.

It took 25,000 100-pound bags of concrete to create the structure over the course of 16 months, at a cost of $100,000 — factoring in inflation, that would amount to nearly $1.45 million in 2019.

Five filters to keep the pool clean cost $50,000.

Swimmers and sunbathers enjoy Liberty Heights in the 1940s.

Instead of a deep end and a shallow end, the pool got deeper as you got closer to the center, with underwater depths of 2 feet for youngsters, 4 feet for older folks who still wanted to touch bottom, and 12 feet at the center, where the three-tier diving platform was situated. It topped out at 20 feet above the surface.

On the lower levels were dressing rooms, lockers and a concession stand. The upper level featured a pavilion with a 16,000-square-foot oak floor for dancing (or roller skating) that could accommodate 500 couples at a time. Unfortunately, the roof blew off the building in 1931, and the dance floor was converted into a sunbathing deck.

Price of admission: A quarter for kids and spectators; twice that for adults.

The pool was still going strong in 1959, when Coca-Cola sponsored a free dance party for teenagers — broadcast on WMVA with disc jockey Jay Holmes — every Friday from 8:30 to 11:30 p.m.

But the end was near.

The pool finally met its demise in 1960, as more families installed their own backyard pools and attendance sagged. Other new public pools were being built, as well: The Druid Hills pool on Indian Trail was already two years old, while the Southside Martinsville Pool on Paul Street and the Villa Heights pool on Beaver Creek Road were both under construction. So was an indoor pool at the Martinsville Community Recreation Center on Cleveland Avenue, which would offer swimming in a meet-size pool year-round.

Four years later, Dorothy Cleal would describe the scene at the abandoned Liberty Heights pool in sadly poetic terms for an article in *The Martinsville Bulletin*:

"Today, a chance footstep echoes along the labyrinth of stone corridors. Locker doors sag and bang in the summer breeze. Weeds and grass push through cracks in cement stairs once crowded with shouting youngsters. Teenage sunbathers who filled the upper level patio with their blankets and portable radios are grown and gone."

The only people still there: a Lester Lumber employee who lived in a first-floor apartment with his wife and six children. The company still used the place to wash logs, and the kids, who ranged in age from 5 months to 10 years, thought it was a blast living in a swimming pool.

It was finally torn down in 1988 to make way for the Liberty Fair Mall.

Baseball

Martinsville has a team in the collegiate summer Coastal Plain League, the Mustangs, who began playing in 2005 and won three consecutive league titles starting in 2009. As of 2019, the league had 16 teams, from southern Virginia down to Georgia, where the Macon Bacon and Savannah Bananas play. (Those are actual team names; no kidding.)

From 1988 to 2003, Martinsville fielded a team in the Appalachian Rookie League, affiliated first with the Philadelphia Phillies and then with the Houston Astros.

Since 1988, Martinsville's baseball pro teams have played at Hooker Field, capacity 3,200, which opened in 1988 at Commonwealth Boulevard and Chatham Heights Road. It's also home to the Patrick Henry Community College Patriots.

But that wasn't Martinsville's first taste of professional baseball. Back in 1934, the aptly named Martinsville Manufacturers played their first season as charter members of the Bi-State League, which fluctuated between six and eight teams during its nine years of existence. (Martinsville fielded a team every year except for the league's final season, 1942.)

The circuit was a Class-D league, which meant you couldn't get any lower on the ladder of organized baseball at the time — Class-D leagues don't even exist anymore. All the league members played in cities and towns within a limited radius of one another, some of them quite small.

Other charter members were the Fieldale Virginians, Danville Leafs, Mt. Airy Graniteers, Mayodan Senators and Leaksville-Draper-Spray Triplets. (That last name was a mouthful; it's easy to see why those three cities consolidated into a single entity in 1967, and adopted the much more compact name Eden.)

The Fieldale entry was later called the Towlers, who in 1936 featured a third baseman named Ken Keltner. A future seven-time All-Star with the Cleveland Indians, Keltner led the Bi-State League in runs (120) and hits (175), hitting .360 on a salary of $40 a month. The rest of the Towlers, however, were awful, and Fieldale finished seventh in the eight-team league.

The ballclub folded following the season.

Other Bi-State League entries over the years included the Bassett Furnituremakers, Mayodan Millers and Reidsville Luckies (for Lucky Strike cigarettes). The Bassett club made it to four consecutive finals starting in 1935, winning three of them — including a 4-3 triumph over Martinsville in 1937 with a ballclub that featured a future Hall of Famer in 19-year-old shortstop Phil Rizzuto.

A Brooklyn native destined for the New York Yankees, Rizzuto recalled his first impression of Bassett: "I get off the train and there's nothing there. I said, 'Where the hell is the town?' Then the train pulled away, and there was the town. There was a drugstore, a post office, and a diner. They had only thirteen hundred people in the whole town. The people were so nice, but they couldn't understand me with my Brooklyn accent, and I couldn't understand them with their Southern accent."

Despite losing in the finals that year, Martinsville had a fairly successful run in the league. Although they never finished at the top of the standings, the Manufacturers made the championship series two other times and won the title in 1940 after finishing second in the regular season.

MARTINSVILLE MEMORIES

They started out playing at Brown Street Field before team owner Jim English built English Field, a ballpark with bleachers and a concrete grandstand. According to one fan's recollection, 5,000 fans attended a playoff game between the Manufacturers and Danville Leafs there in the late 1930s. (English Field was modernized for Appalachian League play and renamed Hooker Field after Hooker Furniture helped fund the upgrade.)

Jimmy Sanders, who also managed the Manufacturers in 1934, won the league's first batting title with a .423 average, the highest of any minor-league player that year. Teammates Joe Concannon and Sam Narron each hit .365. But none of them was the most famous player to pass through Martinsville. That distinction belongs to Enos "Country" Slaughter, who had been born to a tobacco family in Roxboro, North Carolina, just over 60 miles to the southwest.

"We played over on Roy Moore's farm," he said in 2001. "When we cut the wheat, we'd lay out a field, and we'd play baseball. We took beeswax and thread, and sewed our own baseball. Later, we took tape and wrapped it. My dad made me a bat out of a mulberry tree."

Slaughter played his first season of organized ball for the Manufacturers, connecting for 115 hits, including 25 doubles and 18 home runs, in 109 games. He hit .275 and made $75 a month. It turned out to be his only season with the Manufacturers, and three years later, he was playing right field for Martinsville's parent team, the St. Louis Cardinals. A 10-time All-Star and four-time World Series champion, he was inducted into the Hall of Fame in 1985.

The Manufacturers were affiliated with the St. Louis Cardinals for four summers, then with the Phillies for their final two campaigns.

Their 1941 team finished second and failed to make the finals despite a potent lineup that included outfielders Tom Burnette — who led the league in home runs with 29 and RBI with 114 while hitting at a .334 clip and stealing 34 bases — alongside batting champion Albert Behrends (.378). Player-manager George Farrell tied Burnette for the league lead in RBI, while hitting .350 and pacing the circuit with 41 doubles.

Another noteworthy member of that team was shortstop Walter "Tee-Pot" Frye, who hit .278 but was better known as a defensive wizard. Born just 20 miles down the road in Stoneville, North Carolina, Frye was in the first season of what would become a storied minor-league career. Although he never got to the majors, he made such an impact during his 10 minor-league seasons — seven in the Carolina League — that *Sports Illustrated* named him one of North Carolina's top 50 athletes of the 20th century.

Despite its strong showing in 1941, Martinsville didn't field a team in 1942. The whole Bi-State League went out of business after that, bowing to the reality of World War II, and didn't start up again afterward.

But in 1945, the Martinsville Athletics debuted as charter members of the Class-C Carolina League — which is still active today, and which featured the Durham Bulls of *Bull Durham* movie fame among its original teams. (The Leaksville Triplets and Danville Leafs, holdovers from the Bi-State League, were also among the eight teams in the circuit that first year.)

The A's lasted for four seasons, and had a future Hall of Famer in the dugout during their first campaign: Heinie Manush, a Hall of Fame outfielder who compiled a .330 lifetime batting average. Manush only managed the team for one year, but the A's did win a pennant in their next-to-last season, beating the Reidsville Luckies for the title after finishing second in the standings. Eddie Morgan, a former big-leaguer with the St. Louis Browns and Brooklyn Dodgers, managed the team that season.

More recently, 2007 National League MVP Jimmy Rollins got his start as an infielder with the Martinsville Phillies at age 17 in 1996. So did infielder Scott Rolen, who played for Martinsville in 1993. Rolen was the NL Rookie of the Year four years later and went on to be a seven-time All-Star.

Fairs

Swimming wasn't the only activity at Liberty Heights. There was actually an airport, run by the Lester Aviation Co., and the Henry County Fair was held there for a number of years.

The fair got its start way back in 1906 as a three-day event. It appears to have gone on hiatus for a few years — perhaps in deference to World War I — because the 1927 event was called the "fifth annual" county fair. It featured a parade of 25 decorated cars, with a Dodge roadster winning the $50 prize for best "float."

The 1938 fair opened with "fireworks every night," according to *The Martinsville*

MARTINSVILLE MEMORIES

Bulletin, and was apparently an integrated event: The newspaper noted that "invitations are extended to our white and colored friends."

By 1961, the fair's run had expanded to six days, beginning September 4. Family and Children's Days were among the attractions. An ad in *The Bulletin* in 1967 promised a free bicycle would be given away on Children's Day, when all schoolkids would be admitted free until 6 p.m. If they brought the ad to the fair, they'd get eight rides for a buck.

The fair wasn't the only event held at Liberty Heights. In 1965, the Cristiani Wallace Bros. Circus visited the fairgrounds, featuring an elephant named Myrtle and a "herd of pachyderms," high-wire performers, and a horseback-riding act from Belgium, all under a big-top tent. There was even a hippopotamus from Egypt named Miss Eva.

A mural on the Main Street wall of the first Globman's store at the courthouse square shows circus elephants such as those that visited Martinsville in 1965 as part of the Cristiani Wallace Bros. Circus.

Summertime brought another event, the Fireman's Bazaar, which was held at Liberty Heights or the old high school football field.

The Martinsville Volunteer Fire Department sponsored the annual bazaar, and the firefighters would staff the concession stands themselves. The event, which included an auction, served as a fundraiser for the group, which typically brought in $3,000 to $5,000 to purchase things such as fire equipment and a recreational cottage for city employees at Beaver Creek Reservoir.

According to a 1966 article in *The Bulletin*, the events were "noted for their wholesomeness." No "questionable or objectionable displays" were permitted, mischief-makers weren't tolerated and gambling booths were prohibited. As a result, the article said, most of the fair attendees were parents with young children and slightly older youths who enjoyed the rides.

There was an opening-night parade featuring fire engines and other emergency vehicles. There was even a bingo table.

"It was a county fair-type event held annually for a lot of years, up through my 20s, even," Stephen Mark Rainey recalled. "In the '60s, it was set up at Brown Street Field, across from the school (it was the original football field for the old Martinsville High School, where the recycling dumpsters now reside across from the school). It was an exciting thing for me as a kid — they had rides like the Ferris wheel, tilt-a-whirl, bumper cars, that kind of thing."

Today, the old Brown Street Field is no more, like the Broad Street Hotel, the Liberty Heights Pool and the Park Mor Drive-In. But so many other reminders of the past remain in plain view for residents and visitors of Martinsville to enjoy. Part of the joy in writing this book was to seek them out, find them, and share them with you, the reader.

History isn't a collection of dry details from someone else's story. It's the living, evolving chronicle of our shared lives here on this planet. It's our foundation and our legacy. And there's so much of it here in Martinsville, the least we can do is keep it alive.

The Martinsville Dam on the Smith River parallels the Smith River Bridge on Business Route 220. The dam, which was operating by 1924, replaced an old mill dam at the site.

Timeline

1740 — Joseph Martin born.

1749 — Hairston family mansion Marrowbone built in Ridgeway.

1774 — Joseph Martin builds estate on Leatherwood Creek.

1775 — Patrick Henry moves to Leatherwood plantation.

1777 — Henry County formed out of a part of Pittsylvania County.

1790 — Joseph Martin elected to Virginia House of Delegates.

1793 — First courthouse built in Martinsville, then called simply Henry Courthouse.

1795* — George Hairston House built on Jones Street.

The old Axton post office at 193 Axton Road was no longer being used as a post office by 1911 and was later converted into a bank. In 2019, it was operating as Sandy River Pork, selling bacon, hamburgers, pork chops, sausages, eggs, and chicken.

1808 — Greenwood home built near Axton for Joseph Martin III.

1824 — Second courthouse built in Martinsville.

1832 — Horsepasture founded.

1835 — Martinsville population: 84.

1848 — Post office established at Irisburg, also known as Irishburg.

1852 — First post office at Ridgeway established.

1873 — Martinsville incorporates.

1875 — Tobacco Board of Trade set up to regulate tobacco industry in town.

1880 — Martinsville population: 289.

1881 — First train stops in Martinsville on "Dick & Willie" line.

   C.P. Kearfott arrives in town, establishes pharmacy on courthouse square.

1882 — Henry County Bank established.

   Grace United Presbyterian Church built on Fayette Street.

   Post office established at Axton, formerly called "Old Center."

1884 — Spencer adopts current name (formerly Spencer's Store).

1886 — Three men killed in Spencer-Terry gunfight on Fayette Street.

1890 — Martinsville population: approximately 2,000.

1890* — Christ Episcopal Church built on Church Street.

MARTINSVILLE MEMORIES

The original Oak Hall on Church Street, which burned down in 1917, is seen in this vintage postcard. It was replaced on the site by the Rucker-Pannill House, which still stands next to Christ Episcopal Church.

1891 — People's Bank established.

1894 — Little Post Office built.

1900 — Martinsville population: 2,384.

1902 — Bassett Furniture Company established.

1905 — Oak Hall built on Church Street.

1906 — Eight automobiles pass through Martinsville on the Glidden Tour.
American Furniture founded.
Martinsville hosts first Henry County Fair for three days starting Oct. 10.

1910 — Martinsville population: 3,368.
Spencer Penn School built.

1911 — Berlin's Department Store opens on East Main.

1913 — Virginia Mirror Company established.

1914 — Masonic Temple constructed at Church and Bridge streets.

1915 — Globman's Department Store founded.

1917 — Oak Hall destroyed in fire; subsequently rebuilt as Rucker-Pannill House.

1918 — Wedding Cake House built on Starling Avenue.
Shackelford Hospital built on Church Street (originally a Victorian home).

1919* — Fieldale built as company town for Fieldcrest mill.

Liberty Heights Pool is pictured in this postcard courtesy of Martinsville-Henry County Historical Society.

1920 — G.T. Lester builds concrete reservoir containing water from Jones Creek.
   Martinsville population: 4,075
1921 — Work begins on First Baptist Church, Broad and Church streets.
1922 — First United Methodist Church constructed at Church and Lester streets.
   Henry Hotel opens on Church Street.
   Dana Baldwin begins building Baldwin Block on Fayette.
   All-black Martinsville Training School opens on Smith Street.
1924 — Stanley and Hooker furniture companies founded.
   Martinsville Dam completed.
1925 — National Theater built on Church Street.
   Rives S. Brown Sr. begins development along Mulberry Road.
   Pannill Knitting Company founded.
1926 — Dana Baldwin opens St. Mary's Hospital on Fayette Street.
   Liberty Heights Pool built.
1927 — Thomas Jefferson Hotel opens at Church and Bridge streets.
   First Martinsville Colored Fair is held.
1928 — Ohev Zion Synagogue built on Broad Street.
   Broad Street Christian Church built.
1928 — Martinsville becomes an independent city.

MARTINSVILLE MEMORIES

Fairy Stone Park was the largest of six original Virginia state parks that opened in 1936. Philpott Lake in the park, at left, was created with the construction of a dam completed in 1952.

1929 — Main structure on Baldwin Block burns, but the block is rebuilt.
   Dry Bridge School for African-American children opens.
1930 — Martinsville population: 7,705
   Leggett's opens in 7,000-square-foot rental space.
1931 — Roof blows off of Liberty Heights Pavilion.
1934 — Martinsville Manufacturers begin play in baseball's Bi-State League.
1935 — Leggett's Department Store moves to larger building on Church Street.
   Rives Theatre opens.
1936 — Bassett Furniture Makers win first of three straight Bi-State League titles.
   Fairy Stone State Park opens 16 miles northwest of Martinsville.
1937 — Worst flood in history inundates hundreds of Martinsville, Bassett homes.
   Sale Knitting founded.
1938 — Rives S. Brown begins developing Forest Park neighborhood.
1939 — New post office constructed on Church Street.
   New high school (now a middle school) campus built on Cleveland Avenue.
1940 — Martinsville population: 10,080.
   Martinsville defeats Bassett 4 games to 3 for Bi-State League title.
1941 — DuPont factory built on horseshoe bend of Smith River.
1945 — Martinsville A's are charter members of the Carolina League.
   Martinsville Training School renamed Albert Harris School.

Druid Lanes on Spruce Street in its heyday, courtesy of James Coleman. It was the first modern bowling center in Martinsville.

1947 — Martinsville Speedway opens as a dirt track with 750 seats on Sept. 7.
General Hospital constructed on Starling Avenue.
Lynwood Golf and Country Club opens.

1948 — Construction on Philpott Dam, about 20 miles northwest of Martinsville, begins.
First NASCAR-sanctioned race in Martinsville run on July 4.
Martinsville Drive-In opens.
Albert Harris School adds high school grades and curriculum.

1950 — Martinsville population: 17,251.
Globman's moves to larger store on Church Street.

1951 — Seven black men electrocuted after being convicted of raping a white woman.
Warehouse fire on Franklin Street causes $1 million in damage.

1952 — Castle Drive-In opens in Collinsville.
Philpott Dam complete.

1955 — Martinsville Speedway track paved.

1958 — New Albert Harris High School opens on Smith Street.

1959 — Druid Hills Shopping Center opens, anchored by Kroger.

1960 — Richard Petty notches his first of 15 NASCAR wins at Martinsville.
Liberty Heights pool closes.
Druid Lanes built for more than $500,000 on Spruce Street.
Martinsville population: 18,798.
First Baptist Church, Ohev Zion Synagogue move to new buildings.

MARTINSVILLE MEMORIES

Smith River Sports Complex opened in 2009 on Irisburg Road just south of town off Route 58. The $8.7 million complex features two synthetic-turf fields, and three Bermuda grass fields, along with bleachers and a concession stand. It's used for soccer and other recreational events.

1962 — Collinsville Shopping Center opens, anchored by Leggett's and Winn-Dixie.
Sportlanes opens in Collinsville.

1965 — One hundred firefighters battle American Furniture blaze.

1966 — Patrick Henry Mall, anchored by Penney's, opens at Church and Brookdale.
Leggett's moves to new building across from Globman's on Church Street.

1968 — Martinsville schools integrated.
220 Drive-In opens in Collinsville.

1969 — Martinsville High School moves to its current campus.

1970 — Martinsville population: 19,653.
City purchases, demolishes Baldwin Block buildings.*
Martinsville Memorial Hospital opens.

1971 — Sale Knitting becomes Tully Corporation.

1976 — Piedmont Arts Association opens in Lynwood House.
Tully Corporation (formerly Sale Knitting) becomes Tultex.

1979 — Martinsville, Castle drive-ins close.

1980 — Martinsville population: 18,149.

1981 — Piedmont Arts Association moves to former Schottland home on Starling.

1984 — Virginia Museum of Natural History opens in old elementary school.
Movie Town opens on Greensboro Road, Martinsville's first multiplex.

1987 — 220 Drive-In closes.

1988 — First live telecast from Martinsville Speedway: Goody's 500 on ESPN.
  English field ballpark remodeled, reopens as Hooker Field.
1989 — Liberty Fair Mall opens.
1990 — Martinsville population: 16,162.
1998 — DuPont factory closes.
1999 — Tultex files for Chapter 11 bankruptcy protection.
2000 — Martinsville population: 15,416.
  Tultex closes Martinsville plant.
2001 — Hollywood Cinemas opens next to Walmart.
2004 — Virginia Museum of Natural History moves to Starling Avenue location.
2009 — Smith River Sports Complex opens.
2010 — Martinsville population: 13,821.
2012 — Lynwood Golf and Country Club closes.
2013 — Baldwin Building, housing New College Institute, opens on Fayette.
2014 — Liberty Hills Mall converted to outdoor center, Village of Martinsville.
  Six buildings on American Furniture's closed Aaron Street complex burn.
2015 — Walsh's Chicken and More gutted in electrical fire.
2017 — Walsh's reopens in new location on Church Street uptown.
2019 — Rives Theatre burns.
* Date approximate.

Kayaking on the Smith River.
Courtesy of Harvest Foundation

MARTINSVILLE MEMORIES

No, it's not Nessie. But this climbing greenery along the side of Indian Trail in Druid Hills sure makes it seem like a Lake Lanier Monster is on the loose.

Sources

"'70s Dutch Inn Promotional Materials," Second Period Industries, secondperiodindustries.blogspot.com, Nov. 30, 2009.
Adamson, Tola. "City hopes to revive historical hangout spot, Paradise Inn," wset.com, Jan. 5, 2016.
"Alleged Bootlegger Escapes Hospital," Danville Bee, p. 1, Marcy 23, 1922.
"Annual Firemen's Bazaar Merits Support Of Martinsville People," Martinsville Bulletin, June 26, 1966.
"Architectural Survey of Henry County," dhr.virgnia.gov.
"Auto Agency Building To Be Converted To Bowling Alley," Martinsville Bulletin, p. 1, March 29, 1961.
"Auto Race At Martinsville Next Sunday," The Danville Bee, p. B-8, Sept. 1, 1947.
"Automobile Blue Book, Vol. 6, 1921," p. 611.
Baldassaro, Lawrence. "Phil Rizzuto," sabr.org.
Barto, Kim. "Apartment units proposed for factory," Martinsville Bulletin, March 15, 2009.
Baseball-reference.com.
Bassetthistoricalcenter.com.
"Belk, Inc. History," fundinguniverse.com.
"Biographies of Henry County, VA," genealogytrails.com.

"BlackBox Theatre," visitmartinsville.com.

Blanton, Alison S.; Hill, Helen R.; Zirkle, Mary A.; and Marshall, Stacy L. "Historical Architectural Survey of Martinsville Va., Hill Studio, June 1998.

"Blue Ridge Regional Library – Martinsville Branch History," brrl.lib.va.us.

Bonior, Jeffrey. "They Once Had the Best Job in Town. Not Anymore," americanmanufacturing.org, Dec. 11, 2014.

"Bootleggers Adopt Protective Convoy," Richmond Times-Dispatch, p. 2, July 10, 1920.

Bragg, Susan. "Martinsville Seven (1949-1951)," blackpast.org, June 3, 2011.

"Broad Street Hotel in 1919," myhenrycounty.com.

"Carter, John Waddey, House," waymarking.com.

Casey, Dan. "The wettest spot on Earth," Richmond Times-Dispatch, June 17, 2018.

Cinematreasures.org.

"City To Get Big Bowling Center," Martinsville Bulletin, p. 1, March 30, 1960.

Cleal, Dorothy. "Dr. Baldwin Celebrates 50th Year In City," Martinsville Bulletin, p. 7-A, Oct. 16, 1960

Cleal, Dorothy. "Live In A Pool? They Like It," Martinsville Bulletin, p. 1, June 8, 1964.

Cleal, Dorothy. "Martinsville Area Swimming Pools Being Readied To Help Cool Off That Lage Spring Fever," Martinsville Bulletin, p. 9-A, May 15, 1960.

Cleal, Dorothy and Herbert, Hiram H. "Foresight, Founders, and Fortitude," 1970, Bassett Printing Corp., Bassett, Va.

Collins, Paul. "Martinsville fire chief says cause of destructive fire at Rives Theatre's doesn't appear suspicious," Martinsville Bulletin, Sept. 9, 2019.

Cooper, Cara. "Martinsville celebrates 15th state basketball championship," Martinsville Bulletin, March 13, 2016.

Cooper, Cara. "Martinsville holding out hope for final MLB Hall chance," Martinsville Bulletin, Jan. 26, 2008.

"Danville & Western Railway – NS Eden Branch," wvncrails.org.

DeHart, Carl. "An Explosive Day in Martinsville Uptown," visitmartinsville.com.

"Doctors Must Turn To Bootleggers For Medicinal Whisky," Danville Bee, p. 3, Sept. 7, 1922.

Dorsey, Barry. "Looking Back On Southside: The Great Road's impact on Henry County," Martinsville Bulletin, Sept. 11, 2017.

Dorsey, Barry. "Martinsville and Henry County: Three Major Job Transitions and the Future of Jobs, mhchistoricalsociety.org, May 15, 2018.

Driveins.org.

"Driver Listing (Virginia)," racing-reference.info.

"DuPont plant closing brings end of an era," The Dispatch (Davidson County), p. 3B, June 29, 1998.

"Earl Sumner Draper," www-personal.umich.edu.

Eaton, Lorraine. "Virginia's Prohibition history," The Virginian-Pilot, Nov. 30, 2008.

"Encyclopedia of Southern Jewish Communities - Martinsville, Virginia," isjl.org.

"Enjoy Dinner," Danville Bee, p. 6, Dec. 23, 1938.

"Enos Slaughter, Controversial Cardinal," legacy.com.

"Explore the haunted side of the Dan River region," st8crossings.com.

"Fake Bootlegger Obtains $4,000," Danville Bee, p. 3, July 6, 1922.

"A Family in Black and White," 60 Minutes, cbsnews.com.

"Fayette Street," Fayette Area Historical Initiative and Virginia Foundation for the Humanities, 2006.

"Fayette Street history: Churches," Martinsville Bulletin, Oct. 15, 2006.

Fifer, Jordan. "Founder of Kenney's Burger Chain Knew Secret to Keep Customers Coming," The Roanoke Times, July 18, 2012.

"First Baptist Church Martinsville," firstbaptistmartinsville.com.

Flora, Emily. "William Kenney recalls his life as a business man and his work with Habitat for Humanity," The Roanoke Times, July 20, 2009.

"Fieldale Hotel," myhenrycounty.com.

MARTINSVILLE MEMORIES

Fleenor, Lawrence. "General Joseph Martin," danielboontrail.com, January 2001.
"Francis Reid 'Frank' Penn, Sr," findagrave.com.
"Furnishing a Nation," visitmartinsville.com.
"General Joseph Martin, 1740-1808," mhchistoricalsociety.org, Oct. 6, 2009.
Gettleman, Jeffrey. "It's Like Getting Fleeced," Los Angeles Times, Feb. 20, 2002.
"Globman's," mchistoricalsociety.org.
"Gravely History," Ye Olde Gravely, yeoldegravely.com.
Hairston, Douglas. "Dutch Inn tower remains, for now, amid demolition," Martinsville Bulletin, May 29, 2001.
"Hairston Plantations," afrovirginia.org.
Hall, Debbie. "Members call clubs closing bittersweet," Martinsville Bulletin, Jan. 1, 2012.
"A Harmful Influence on Industry," Danville Bee, p. 6, Oct. 29, 1923.
"Henry County Fair," Richmond Times Dispatch, p. 5, Oct. 6, 1906.
"Henry County's Hensley inducted into VA Motorsports Hall," Martinsville Bulletin, Aug. 27, 2018.
"Henry Fair Is Well Attended," Danville Bee, p. 5, Sept. 24, 1926.
"Henry Uptown," eschelonresourcesinc.com.
"Hensley gets inducted into Va. HOF class," Martinsville Bulletin, April 17, 2013.
Hill, Judith Parks America. "A History of Henry County, Virginia," Heritage Books, 2008 (originally published in 1925).
"The Historic Bassett Train Depot," virginia.org.
"Historic Carolina Road Through Henry County," virginia.org.
"Historic Henry County Courthouse," mhchistoricalsociety.org.
"Historic John D Bassett Event Center," virginia.org.
"A History of Roads in Virginia: Most Convenient Wayes," Virginia Department of Transportation, virginiadot.org, 2006.
"History of Roanoke," visitroanokeva.com.
"The History of Spencer-Penn," thecentreatspencerpenn.com.
"History of Virginia, Vol. VI: Virginia Biography," American Historical Society, Chicago and New York, 1924.
"Hooker Field, Martinsville, Virginia," littleballparks.com.
"Hooker Furniture," hookerfurniture.com.
"The Horseless Age," p. 106, July 25, 1906.
"The 'horseless carriage' comes to Henry County," Martinsville Bulletin, Sept. 10, 2018.
Horton, Laurel. "An Upcountry Legacy: Mary Black's Family Quilts," southernspaces.org, May 19, 2006.
"How to Chew Tobacco," wikihow.com.
"Junior Deputy League To Sponsor Circus Here," Martinsville Bulletin, p. 7, April 7, 1965.
Kazek, Kelly. "7 southern wedding-cake houses, plus 1 eye-popping church," al.com.
Keiper, Joe; Boaz, Noel; and Leavitt, Russell. "The Good Doctors Shackelford," The Martinsville Bulletin, March 9, 2017.
King, Virginia. "Do you remember when Martinsville had a concrete pool?" Martinsville Bulletin, July 14, 2018.
King, Virginia. "The Jewish Community in Martinsville," Martinsville Bulletin, May 11, 2017.
Kozelsky, Holly. "50 YEARS: Piedmont Arts celebrates half-century mark," Martinsville Bulletin, Oct. 2011.
Kritzer, Jamie. "Magazine lauds Stoneville baseball legend," Greensboro News & Record, p. B1, Jan. 3, 2000.
"Large Crowd at Movie Opening," Danville Bee, p. 8, Oct. 10, 1935.
"Liberty Fair Mall," triposo.com.
"Liberty Heights Pool: History of service, fun," Martinsville Bulletin, Oct. 16, 2008
"Lynwood Golf Club — Martinsville, VA," golflink.com.
"Martin, General Joseph," genealogytrails.org.
"Martinsville and Henry County Historic Driving Tour," Martinsville-Henry County Historical Society brochure.
"Martinsville Branch History," Blue Ridge Regional Library, brrl.lib.va.us.
"Martinsville Novelty Corporation Factory," National Register of Historic Places Registration Form, dhr.virginia.gov.

STEPHEN H. PROVOST

"Martinsville, Virginia Ghost Sightings," ghostsofamerica.com.

Maxpreps.com.

McCormick, Steve. "Oldest NASCAR Sprint Cup Race Tracks," liveabout.com, Feb. 12, 2019.

"Memorial Hospital of Martinsville and Henry County and Danville Regional Medical Center Become SOVAH Health," Martinsvillehospital.com, June 8, 2017.

"MHC Garden Day: 3 neighborhoods, 3 worlds," visitmartinsville.com, March 19, 2019.

"NASCAR Rooted in Prohibition Bootlegging," prohibition.themobmuseum.org.

"New $800,000 Collinsville Shopping Center To Open At 10 A.M. Wednesday," Martinsville Bulletin, April 10, 1962.

"New Kroger Store Set To Open," Staunton News-Leader, p. 4, Jan. 11, 1959.

"New Penney Store Opens Thursday," Martinsville Bulletin, p. 1, Jan. 5, 1966.

Nitz, Jim. "Ken Keltner," sabr.org.

"Norfolk and Western Railway, Precision Transportation," american-rails.com.

Perry, Thomas D. "Images of Martinsville Virginia," Laurel Hill Publishing, Ararat, Virginia, 2009.

Perry, Tom. "Shootout on Fayette Street," freestateofpatrick.blogspot.com, March 18, 2010.

Phccpatriotplayers.com.

Powell, Mickey. "Construction finally starts on new museum facility," Martinsville Bulletin, June 15, 2004.

Powell, Mickey. "Factory Inferno: Former American building burn," Martinsville Bulletin, March 5, 2014.

Powell, Mickey. "Fire damages American furniture facility in Martinsville," Martinsville Bulletin, April 22, 2017.

Powell, Mickey. "Former News-Post publisher turns hobby into business," Martinsville Bulletin, Dec. 28, 2010.

Powell, Mickey. "Local Kmart to close in December," Martinsville Bulletin, Sept. 20, 2016.

Powell, Mickey. "Mall seeks improvements, tenants," Martinsville Bulletin, Nov. 23, 2012.

Powell, Mickey. "The Henry is set to make its debut," Martinsville Bulletin, July 28, 2015.

Prillaman, H. Arnold. "Baseball not supported," Martinsville Bulletin, Sept. 7, 2007.

"Red Byron Wins 100-Mile Stock Car Race," Atlanta Constitution, p. 7, Sept. 26, 1949.

Reif, Rita. "The Little Virginia Town That Thrives on Making Furniture," The New York Times, Jan. 10, 1970.

"Restaurant To Be Built On Boulevard," Martinsville Bulletin, p. 2, Aug. 17, 1964.

"Ridgeway, Virginia Ghost Sightings," ghostsofamerica.com.

Roosterwalk.com.

Ross, John. "Henry Hotel: Good Years And Lean Years," Martinsville Bulletin, May 1, 1966.

Ross, Pat and Snead, Fran. "History Corner," bassetthistoricalcenter.com, Sept. 6, 2007.

Rheinheimer, Kurt. "Roanoke in 1931," The Roanoker, Sept. 1, 2009.

Rucker, Steve. "The Tobacco Industry in the City of Martinsville and Henry County," mhchistoricalsociety.org.

"Sam Lions Trail keeps up talk of legend," Martinsville Bulletin, May 11, 2003.

"Schlosser, Jim. "Book Retells One Name, Two Worlds," Greensboro News & Record, April 2, 1999.

Selko, Jamie. "Minor League All-Star Teams, 1922-1962," McFarland & Company, Jefferson, N.C. and London, 2007.

"Senior PBA to make first stop in area," Martinsville Bulletin, July 17, 2008.

Smith, Eric Ledell. "African American Theater Buildings: An Illustrated Directory, 1900-1955," McFarland & Co., Jefferson, N.C., and London.

"Smith River Bridge," bridgehunter.com.

"Star Routes," about.usps.com.

"The Stroller," Martinsville Bulletin, p. 1, Aug. 2, 1967.

Summers, Lewis Preston. "History of Southwest Virginia, 1746-1786, Washington County, 1777-1870," J.L. Hill Printing Co., Richmond, Va., 1903.

"A Terrible Affray," Richmond Dispatch, p. 3, May 18, 1886.

"The Grey Lady," virginia.org.

"Theatre Case Is Heard in Court," Danville Bee, p. 7, Sept. 29, 1936.

MARTINSVILLE MEMORIES

"TheatreWorks Community Players," twcp.net.

Thompson, K.L. Jr. "Fire Heavily Damages Furniture Plant Here," Martinsville Bulletin, p. 1, Feb. 24, 1965.

"Track Timeline," martinsvillespeedway.com.

"Tultex Corporation History," fundinguniverse.com.

Tupponce, Joan. "Old Tultex mill finds new life as office space," virginiabusiness.com, Nov. 30, 2011.

"Two Officers Defend Their Recent Action," Danville Bee, p. 1, Feb. 24, 1925.

Tyree, Elizabeth, and Pinto, Caren. "Wedding Cake House in Martinsville goes up for sale," wset.com, June 21, 2017.

"The Valley Turnpike Company," nps.gov.

"Virginia Mirror announces Expansion," yesmartinsville.com, March 13, 2018.

"Virginia Museum of Natural History," vmnh.net.

"Walking Tour of Historic Fieldale," brochure.

"Watt Harden Hairston," hairston.org.

"What's happening to bowling?" whitehutchison.com.

Wilson, Leonard. "Henry Clay Lester," files.usgwarchives.net.

Williams, Ben R. "Learning more about 'Big Mike,'" June 27, 2018.

Williams, Ben R. "Martinsville takes steps to restore People's Cemetery," Nov. 4, 2017.

Williams, Ben R. "Mural will highlight former site of Walsh's restaurant,'" Sept. 15, 2016.

Williams, Ben R. "Unemployment rate reaches 18-year low in Henry County," June 27, 2018.

Williams, Ben R. "Walsh's a total loss after blaze," Martinsville Bulletin, Sept. 23, 2015.

Williams, Ben R. "Walsh's set to reopen in Martinsville," Martinsville Bulletin, Jan. 28, 2017.

"Winn, Horatio Daniel 1868-1928," The Henry Bulletin, p. 1, Aug. 7, 1928.

"Winn-Dixie To Open Third Store In City And County," Martinsville Bulletin, p. 12, April 10, 1962.

Winston, Elizabeth. "Sign removed from Fayette inn; to be displayed at FAHI," Martinsville Bulletin, Oct. 13, 2010.

Young, Chase. "Osgood sets record with near-perfect series," Martinsville Bulletin, Nov. 5, 2009.

About the author

Stephen H. Provost is an author and historian who has written several books about life in 20th century America. During more than three decades in journalism, he has worked as a managing editor, copy desk chief, columnist and reporter at five newspapers. Now a full-time author, he has written on such diverse topics as American highways, dragons, mutant superheroes, mythic archetypes, language, department stores and his hometown. He currently lives in Martinsville. And he loves cats. Read his blogs and keep up with his activities at stephenhprovost.com.

Did you enjoy this book?

Recommend it to a friend. And please consider rating it and/or leaving a brief review online at Amazon, Barnes & Noble and Goodreads.

Also by the author

Works of Fiction

    The Memortality Saga
        Memortality
        Paralucidity
    The Only Dragon
    Identity Break
    Feathercap
    Nightmare's Eve

Works of Nonfiction

    A Whole Different League
    The Great American Shopping Experience (Fall 2020)
    Highway 99: The History of California's Main Street
    Highway 101: The History of El Camino Real (Spring 2020)
    Fresno Growing Up
    The Legend of Molly Bolin
    Undefeated
    The Phoenix Chronicles
        The Osiris Testament
        The Way of the Phoenix
        The Gospel of the Phoenix
    The Phoenix Principle
        Forged in Ancient Fires
        Messiah in the Making
    Please Stop Saying That!

STEPHEN H. PROVOST

Praise for other works

"The complex idea of mixing morality and mortality is a fresh twist on the human condition. ... **Memortality** is one of those books that will incite more questions than it answers. And for fandom, that's a good thing."
— Ricky L. Brown, Amazing Stories

"Punchy and fast paced, **Memortality** reads like a graphic novel. ... (Provost's) style makes the trippy landscapes and mind-bending plot points more believable and adds a thrilling edge to this vivid crossover fantasy."
— Foreword Reviews

"The genres in this volume span horror, fantasy, and science-fiction, and each is handled deftly. ... **Nightmare's Eve** should be on your reading list. The stories are at the intersection of nightmare and lucid dreaming, up ahead a signpost ... next stop, your reading pile. Keep the nightlight on."
— R.B. Payne, Cemetery Dance

"**Memortality** by Stephen Provost is a highly original, thrilling novel unlike anything else out there."
— David McAfee, bestselling author of 33 A.D., 61 A.D., and 79 A.D.

"Profusely illustrated throughout, **Highway 99** is unreservedly recommended as an essential and core addition to every community and academic library's California History collections."
— California Bookwatch

"An essential primer for anyone seeking an entrée into the genre. Provost serves up a smorgasbord of highlights gleaned from his personal memories of and research into the various nooks and crannies of what 'used-to-be' in professional team sports."
— Tim Hanlon, Good Seats Still Available, on **A Whole Different League**

"As informed and informative as it is entertaining and absorbing, **Fresno Growing Up** is very highly recommended for personal, community, and academic library 20th Century American History collections."

— John Burroughs, Reviewer's Bookwatch

"Provost sticks mostly to the classics: vampires, ghosts, aliens, and even dragons. But trekking familiar terrain allows the author to subvert readers' expectations. ... Provost's poetry skillfully displays the same somber themes as the stories. ... Worthy tales that prove external forces are no more terrifying than what's inside people's heads."

— Kirkus Reviews on **Nightmare's Eve**

"... an engaging narrative that pulls the reader into the story and onto the road. ... I highly recommend **Highway 99: The History of California's Main Street**, whether you're a roadside archaeology nut or just someone who enjoys a ripping story peppered with vintage photographs."

— Barbara Gossett,
Society for Commercial Archaeology Journal

www.ingramcontent.com/pod-product-compliance
Lightning Source LLC
Chambersburg PA
CBHW081916170426
43200CB00014B/2750